WHAT I ATE FOR
BREAKFAST

WHAT I ATE FOR
BREAKFAST

RECIPES WORTH GETTING OUT OF BED FOR

Emily Scott

HarperCollins*Publishers*

HarperCollins*Publishers*
1 London Bridge Street
London SE1 9GF

www.harpercollins.co.uk

HarperCollins*Publishers*
1st Floor, Watermarque Building, Ringsend Road
Dublin 4, Ireland

First published by HarperCollins*Publishers* 2022

10 9 8 7 6 5 4 3 2 1

A catalogue record of this book is available from
the British Library

ISBN 978-0-00-851789-2

Design by Louise Leffler

Printed and bound in Latvia

WHEN USING KITCHEN APPLIANCES PLEASE
ALWAYS FOLLOW THE MANUFACTURER'S
INSTRUCTIONS

MIX
Paper from
responsible sources
FSC™ C007454

www.fsc.org

CONTENTS

INTRODUCTION

ABOUT ME

As a foodie and a self-taught home cook from Suffolk, breakfast has been my favourite meal of the day for as long as I can remember. I have many wonderful memories of staying with both sets of grandparents during school holidays, which happened frequently as my parents worked full-time. I adored my Nan's cooking, in particular her breakfasts. The three of us would gather around the kitchen table and she would spoil us with two breakfast courses, minimum!

My favourite breakfast was her 'dippy eggs' with perfectly cooked yolks, served with toast soldiers for dipping, shortly followed by more hot buttered toast, generously spread with plum jam. Absorbing every moment of the morning ritual, I would watch my Grandad take great care peeling the shell from the top of a boiled egg with the handle of a teaspoon to avoid burning his fingers and would count the number of teaspoons of brown sugar he added to his bowl of porridge (he once got up to seven teaspoons, much to Nan's disapproval!). Whether I was enjoying a scrambled egg sandwich on freshly baked bread, or peanut butter and jam on toast served on my Dad and Uncle's old Batman plate, breakfast time was always special at both my grandparents' homes.

I was able to enhance my cookery skills while studying economics at university and living away from home, making tasty, easy (and economical) meals to fit my student budget. In fact, I probably spent more time in the kitchen than I did in the university library! Although I enjoyed my degree, my true passion (and distraction) has always been cooking . . . and eating the results, of course.

In April 2015, while working full-time, I launched my Instagram page @whatiateforbreakfast, where I began to share my breakfast and brunch recipes, thinking outside the cereal box and coming up with creative, fun and delicious ideas in the hope of inspiring others to make time for breakfast themselves. Despite having no culinary training or background in the food industry, I am immensely proud to have amassed a following of more than 190,000 fellow breakfast-lovers over the past seven years, and have shared over 2,000 breakfast posts on my page to date.

WHY BREAKFAST?

Let's face it, breakfast tends to be the most rushed and least inspired meal due to the majority of us being time-poor and over-tired . . . and that's if we remember to eat it in the first place! My mission in writing this book is to take us back to when breakfast was the most important meal of the day, but also to bring it into the 21st century. Move over soggy cornflakes and plain toast; I aim to shake up the traditional foods that we typically eat in the morning with my innovative, scrumptious ideas using uncomplicated and easy to find ingredients that give you a reason to jump out of bed instead of pressing the snooze button.

My goal is to encourage both novice and experienced home cooks, as well as those who may be breakfast-shy, to rustle up something mouth-watering at the beginning of the day. The book includes sweet and savoury breakfast and brunch dishes, to fit any morning and suit any cooking ability, as well as my advice on how to perfect some of the breakfast essentials, such as eggs and pancakes. Many of the recipes serve one person, but can easily be scaled up if required, so whether you live alone, have a large family, are a student, a busy professional or retired, there is a breakfast for everyone.

The book is divided into the following chapters:

Breakfast Basics and Simple Starters

How to prepare breakfast staples, such as scrambled, poached and soft-boiled eggs, homemade hash browns and fluffy pancakes. This chapter also includes a handful of simple breakfasts, such as Duckpond (egg-in-a-hole) and Frumpets (French toast crumpets) to get you started.

Breakfast to Go

Recipes that can be prepared ahead of time for a speedy breakfast eaten at home or taken with you on the move.

Everyday Breakfasts

Breakfasts that can be enjoyed during the week, with a maximum preparation time of 25 minutes or less.

Lazy Days and Sundays

Dishes for relaxed weekend breakfasts and indulgent brunches, holidays, celebrations or special occasions.

Sprinkled through the book are my top tips and alternatives to encourage you to be adaptable, which will hopefully enable you to give the recipes your own stamp. Whether you are looking for a breakfast to take with you to work and eat 'al-desko', a leisurely weekend brunch, or something in between, it is always possible to start your day in a positive way. Happy breakfast!

I adored my Nan's cooking, in particular her breakfasts. The three of us would gather around the kitchen table and she would spoil us with two breakfast courses, minimum!

MY STORE CUPBOARD, FRIDGE and FREEZER ESSENTIALS

What do I keep in my kitchen to make breakfast time easy? Here's my guide to the ultimate, well-stocked breakfast store cupboard, fridge and freezer that will mean you can rustle up something yummy in the morning, even if you think that you have nothing in!

SEASONINGS, HERBS AND SPICES

Choosing the right seasonings, herbs and spices makes the difference between a boring, bland breakfast and one that wakes up your taste buds. Buying lots of herbs and spices all in one go can be expensive and confusing for a novice cook, so my advice would be to find a handful of your favourites, then gradually build from there. A jar of mixed herbs, such as herbes de Provence or Italian herbs, can cover all bases if you are unsure which ones to buy. Ground cinnamon is probably my most used spice as it adds depth and warmth to dishes: it can be sprinkled on top of porridge, added to pancakes, French toast or muffins, and also works well in tomato-based dishes. Harissa paste is another of my favourites in terms of both flavour and versatility; you can brush halloumi with it before pan-frying, mix it into vegetable fritters and homemade hash browns, or add a spoonful to baked beans for a spicy kick. These are the essentials I'd suggest you buy.

- ★ Sea salt and black pepper
- ★ Dried herbs, such as rosemary, thyme, oregano or chives
- ★ Ground cinnamon and nutmeg
- ★ Garam masala
- ★ Paprika (smoked or unsmoked)
- ★ Chilli powder or chilli flakes
- ★ Harissa paste

DRIED GOODS

- ★ Rolled oats
- ★ Plain and self-raising flour
- ★ Baking powder
- ★ Caster or granulated sugar
- ★ Icing sugar
- ★ Vanilla extract
- ★ Chocolate chips
- ★ Dried fruit and desiccated coconut
- ★ Nuts and seeds
- ★ Tea and coffee

TINS, CONDIMENTS, JARS AND BOTTLES

These are not just for slathering on toast – you can also stir sweet spreads into porridge, use them to top pancakes, waffles and French toast, or even add a spoonful to create a melting centre in baked muffins. Runny honey and maple syrup are useful, natural sources of sweetness, while white wine vinegar is key for poaching eggs (see page 19 for my method). Table sauces, such as ketchup, tend to be cupboard essentials, but sweet chilli sauce is my preferred condiment – it's fantastic served with halloumi, bacon or hash browns.

★ Sweet and savoury spreads such as marmalade, jam, peanut butter, Nutella, Lotus Biscoff and Marmite

★ Runny honey and/or maple syrup

★ Oil suitable for frying and roasting, such as olive oil or cold-pressed rapeseed oil

★ White wine vinegar

★ Table sauces and condiments such as ketchup, brown sauce, sweet chilli sauce or hot sauce

★ Pesto

★ Baked beans

BAKERY

★ Bread and pastries, such as sliced bread, crumpets, croissants, bagels, English muffins, pitta or flatbreads, hot cross buns (see overleaf for my tip on freezing these items)

FRESH FOOD

★ Large free-range eggs

★ Milk (or a non-dairy alternative)

★ Butter

★ Cheese such as halloumi, mature Cheddar, mozzarella or Parmigiano Reggiano

★ Double cream or crème fraîche

★ Bacon (smoked or unsmoked)

★ Potatoes and sweet potatoes

★ Vegetables (I usually have spring onions, baby spinach, mixed peppers, courgettes and carrots in my fridge)

★ Avocados (if yours are taking ages to ripen, speed them up by popping them in the fruit bowl next to the bananas)

★ Fruit such as bananas, apples, pears, peaches or oranges

★ Lemons and limes

★ Fresh herbs, such as basil, chives, coriander, rosemary, oregano or sage (these can all easily be grown in your garden, in containers, or even on your kitchen windowsill, to cut as you need, making them more convenient and cheaper than buying packs from the supermarket)

FROZEN FOOD

Your freezer is an excellent way to store some of the breakfast staples, preventing waste and saving you time and money. You can keep leftovers from recipes (the general rule is that leftovers are safe to freeze for up to three months) to defrost and reheat at a later date, which is ideal for a busy morning when you may be tempted to skip breakfast. My favourite freezer tip is to look out for reduced bakery items, such as sliced bread and crumpets, when visiting the supermarket. You can put them in the freezer as soon as you get home, then use only what you need for each meal. I suggest that you slice items such as bagels, English muffins or hot cross buns in half before freezing them. That way, you can pop them straight into the toaster without having to defrost them first – much easier!

★ Bread and pastries (see above)

★ Bags of frozen fruit such as blueberries, raspberries or cherries (these are great for adding to porridge, pancakes, yoghurt and smoothies or smoothie bowls, so I always have a couple of different types on the go. You can also freeze fresh fruit if you are unable to eat it before it is past its best, for example, ripe bananas – just peel and slice them before freezing)

★ Fresh herbs (wash and finely chop herbs then put in an ice-cube tray and top with a little cold water or olive oil to cover the herbs. Alternatively, you can mix chopped herbs with softened butter and crushed garlic, then store portions of flavoured butter in an ice-cube tray)

KITCHEN EQUIPMENT

This is not a definitive list, but here is a list of the main kitchen items I use throughout the book, as well as when cooking breakfast in general.

★ Small, medium and large non-stick frying pans (16–18cm, 20–24cm and 26–28cm in diameter should cover all bases)

★ Small, medium and large saucepans (14–16cm, 18cm and 20cm in diameter)

★ Utensils, including a slotted spoon, wooden spoon, fish slice, silicone spatula and a hand whisk (an electric hand whisk is also useful for cooking cloud eggs, see page 22, and fluffy pancakes, see page 24)

★ Knives: a paring knife, small cook's knife, large cook's knife and a bread knife are my most used knives

★ Crinkle knife or cutter (see page 28 for how I use this to slice halloumi)

★ Chopping boards (use separate boards for raw meat, raw fish, cooked meat, bread, fruit and vegetables)

★ Kitchen scissors

★ Cheese grater

★ Garlic crusher

★ Spiraliser (or you can use a vegetable peeler for a similar effect)

★ Kitchen scales

★ Blender

★ Waffle iron

- ★ Measuring jug
- ★ Measuring spoons (for accuracy, as cutlery can vary in shape and size)
- ★ Large mixing bowl
- ★ 12-hole non-stick muffin tin
- ★ 900g non-stick loaf tin
- ★ 20cm non-stick springform cake tin
- ★ Large baking dish
- ★ Ramekins or individual baking dishes
- ★ Non-stick baking trays or sheets

- ★ Wire cooling rack
- ★ Baking paper
- ★ Storage boxes or reusable bags for storing leftovers
- ★ Kitchen paper (not just for mopping up spills, but also to drain excess water when poaching eggs, see page 19)
- ★ Tea towels (you can also use these to squeeze the excess liquid from grated potato when making hash browns, see pages 27, 109 and 138)
- ★ Egg cups

BREAKFAST BASICS
and
SIMPLE STARTERS

SILKY
SCRAMBLED EGGS

Step away from the microwave! If you like your scrambled eggs silky and soft, then cooking them on the hob is key. This requires a little extra effort, but gives you more control over the temperature and texture and never results in rubbery eggs. In refining my scrambled egg technique, I have found two pieces of kitchen equipment to be particularly useful: the first is a non-stick frying pan, as the coating prevents the eggs from sticking and overcooking; and the second a silicone spatula, which can be used to scrape excess egg from the sides of the pan while they cook and is flexible enough to gently stir and push the eggs around. A wooden spoon is fine if you don't have a spatula to hand.

Serves 1 | Preparation time: 5–10 minutes

½ tsp butter or oil for frying, such as olive oil or cold-pressed rapeseed oil

2 large free-range eggs

pinch each of salt and freshly ground black pepper

½ tbsp double cream or crème fraîche and ½ tbsp chives, finely chopped, to garnish (optional)

1. Heat the butter in a non-stick frying pan over a medium heat. Use a small or medium-sized frying pan (about 19–22cm in diameter, ideally). You're more likely to overcook the eggs in a larger pan because of the bigger surface area.

2. Once the butter has melted, crack the eggs directly into the pan, then add a pinch of salt. Turn the heat down to low, then use a spatula (or a wooden spoon) to gently push the eggs from the edges of the pan into the centre, using a clockwise motion. The uncooked egg will run into the gaps you create, so repeat this motion until the eggs are nearly cooked.

3. Optional step: at this point, you could stir in the double cream or crème fraîche for extra creamy scrambled eggs.

4. Just before the eggs are cooked to your preferred texture, remove them from the heat. They will carry on cooking in the residual heat of the pan while you serve them, so by the time you tuck into them they will be perfectly cooked. Garnish with a pinch of freshly ground black pepper and the chopped chives, if using, then serve straight away.

Top Tip   When cooking scrambled eggs, I usually don't bother to whisk the eggs beforehand, as they are mixed up in the pan anyway and this means less clearing up afterwards! If you prefer, you can whisk the eggs before heating the pan.

DELICIOUSLY
DIPPY EGGS

Comforting and quick to prepare, my favourite breakfast has to be dippy eggs, in other words, soft-boiled eggs served with toast soldiers. They bring back fond memories of the legendary dippy eggs that my Nan would make for breakfast whenever I stayed with my grandparents. The eggs were always boiled perfectly, with a set white and a runny yolk for dipping the buttery toast soldiers. She would take the eggs out of the fridge the night before, which not only speeds up the cooking time, but also helps to prevent the shells from cracking when putting them in boiling water, so give it a try if you encounter this problem. The timing is crucial; make sure you use a timer to keep track, so you don't end up with disappointingly under- or over-cooked eggs!

Serves 1 | Preparation time: 10 minutes

1 or 2 large free-range eggs

1 medium slice of white or wholemeal bread

10g butter

1. Fill a medium-sized saucepan with enough water to cover the eggs, then bring the water to the boil over a high heat. To speed this up, you can use freshly boiled water from the kettle – I like to make a cup of tea at the same time as it will be brewed just in time to serve with the eggs and soldiers!

2. Once the water has reached a rolling boil (large vigorous bubbles) slowly lower your eggs into the saucepan using a slotted spoon. Keep the water on a rolling boil throughout the cooking and set a timer to cook the eggs for exactly 5 minutes if they're at room temperature, or for exactly 6 minutes if they are straight from the fridge.

3. While the eggs are boiling, toast the bread to your liking, then spread it with butter and slice it into strips.

4. Carefully lift the eggs out of the pan using a slotted spoon, immediately place them in egg cups, then remove the tops. My preferred method is my Grandad's trick: tap the top of the egg with a teaspoon to crack the shell, use the handle of the teaspoon as a lever to peel the shell from the top half of the egg, then turn the teaspoon round again and use it to slice off the top of the egg.

5. Serve the eggs with the toast soldiers and start dipping!

Top Tip **Take your dippy eggs up a notch by swapping the toast soldiers for something more adventurous. There are two super-soldier ideas in this book: smoky sweet potato hash brown soldiers on page 94 and maple thyme-roasted carrot soldiers on page 134, both of which are scrumptious alternatives to toast.**

Top Tip

When poaching eggs, make sure you use the freshest eggs possible. The proteins in egg white deteriorate over time, resulting in those annoying, wispy bits of white when you cook with older eggs.

PERFECT
POACHED EGGS

Poached eggs can be notoriously tricky to crack (if you'll excuse the pun), so here's a method that I've tried and tested over the years to get perfect eggs every time, with no gadgets, cling film or stirring required. All you need is a saucepan of boiling water, free-range eggs, white wine vinegar and a pinch of salt. Adding the vinegar and salt to the boiling water creates tiny bubbles that help to bring the egg white up around the yolk, meaning there's no need to create a whirlpool in the water before adding the eggs. I recommend using white wine vinegar or white vinegar as although malt, cider or red wine vinegar also work, they can discolour the egg white. You can poach several eggs at a time, but I advise poaching no more than two or three eggs per saucepan of water to avoid overcrowding.

Serves 1 | Preparation time: 5–10 minutes

1 or 2 large free-range eggs

½ tbsp white wine vinegar

pinch of salt

1. Fill a medium-sized saucepan with at least 5cm of water, then bring the water to the boil over a high heat (you can use freshly boiled water from the kettle to speed this up). Once the water has reached a rolling boil (large, vigorous bubbles) add the vinegar followed by the salt. Carefully crack the eggs into the water, as close to the surface as possible, then immediately turn down the heat so the water is simmering (small gentle bubbles).

2. Simmer the eggs for exactly 3 minutes if they are at room temperature, or exactly 4 minutes if they are straight from the fridge.

3. Once the time is up, remove the eggs from the water with a slotted spoon and place them on some kitchen paper to absorb any extra water before serving.

FABULOUS
FRIED EGGS

Frying an egg without under- or over-cooking it, or breaking the yolk can be difficult. My method is to fry the eggs slowly over a low heat, which allows enough time for the white to cook while ensuring that the yolk stays runny, so you don't need to flip the egg. Give it a try!

Serves 1 | Preparation time: 5 minutes

1 tsp oil for frying, such as olive oil or cold-pressed rapeseed oil

1 or 2 large free-range eggs

1. Heat the oil in a non-stick frying pan over a medium heat.

2. Once the oil is hot, crack the eggs directly into the pan, then turn the heat down to low. Fry the eggs for 3 minutes, then check to see if the white is cooked to your liking. If not, continue to fry for a further minute. You can also cover the pan with a lid, which will speed up the cooking time by steaming the top of the eggs.

3. Once the white is cooked through but the yolk still runny, carefully lift the eggs out of the pan using a fish slice or spatula and serve immediately.

Top Tip

Swap the oil for a teaspoon of green or red pesto for pesto fried eggs.

CLOUD
EGGS

Cloud eggs may have been a social media trend in 2017, but I'm bringing them into 2022 with this yummy Parmesan and bacon version. Whisking the white gives it a fluffy, cloud-like texture which surrounds the runny yolk. Using an electric whisk, instead of whisking by hand, will save time and prevent your arm from becoming too tired, unless you fancy a morning workout of course!

Serves 1 | Preparation time: 15–20 minutes

1 large free-range egg

pinch of salt and freshly ground black pepper

20g Parmigiano Reggiano cheese, finely grated

20g unsmoked or smoked bacon lardons, or 2 rashers streaky bacon, diced

½ tbsp chives, finely chopped (optional)

1. Preheat your oven to 200°C/ 180°C fan/gas mark 6. Line a baking tray with baking paper.

2. Separate the egg white from the yolk, then set the yolk aside. Put the egg white into a large, clean mixing bowl, then beat it using an electric whisk until it forms stiff peaks.

3. Gently fold the salt, pepper and grated cheese into the egg white, making sure not to knock out too much of the air you whisked in. Spoon the mixture into a circular shape on the baking tray, then use the back of the spoon to create a small well in the centre.

4. Bake for 7–8 minutes, or until the egg white has set and is starting to turn golden.

5. While the egg white is baking, heat a small non-stick frying pan over a medium heat. Once the pan is hot, add the bacon, then fry for 3–4 minutes, or until the lardons are crispy and completely cooked through. Set aside.

6. Remove the egg white from the oven and carefully put the yolk into the well in the centre without breaking it. Return the egg to the oven for a further 3 minutes.

7. Transfer the cloud egg to a plate using a fish slice or spatula. Sprinkle the bacon and chopped chives, if using, over the top, then serve. You can enjoy the cloud egg as it is, or serve it on a slice of toast or a toasted crumpet, both of which are marvellous for mopping up the yolk.

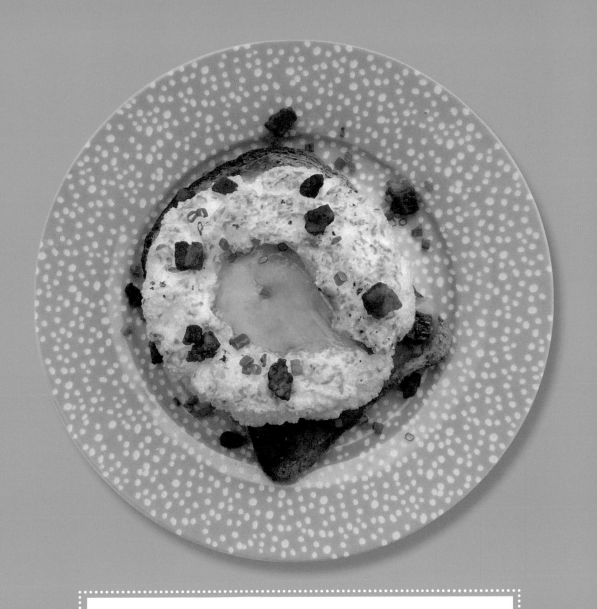

Top Tip Swap the bacon for diced chorizo and add ¼ teaspoon of chilli powder to the egg white for a spicy alternative.

FLUFFY
PANCAKES

There's nothing better than a stack of warm fluffy pancakes for breakfast, drizzled with maple syrup and topped with blueberries. My trick for achieving light and airy American-style pancakes (as opposed to thin, crêpe-style pancakes) is to separate the egg yolk from the white and then whisk the white until it forms stiff peaks – in the same way as you make meringue – before folding it into the pancake batter. The extra step is completely worth it and gives you the fluffiest, cloud-like stack. Once you try cooking pancakes this way, you'll never skip whisking the egg white again!

Serves 1 | Preparation time: 15–20 minutes

40g self-raising flour

½ tsp granulated sugar

½ tsp vanilla extract

60ml semi-skimmed milk (or a non-dairy alternative)

1 large free-range egg

½ tsp oil for frying, such as coconut oil or cold-pressed rapeseed oil

½ tsp icing sugar

½ tbsp maple syrup

80g blueberries

1. Put the flour, sugar, vanilla extract and milk into a large mixing bowl, then stir until combined.

2. Separate the egg, mixing the yolk into the batter. Put the egg white into a separate mixing bowl, then beat it using an electric whisk until it forms stiff peaks. Gently fold the egg white into the pancake batter, making sure not to knock out too much of the air you've whisked in.

3. Heat the oil in a large non-stick frying pan over a medium heat. Once the oil is hot, spoon the batter into the pan, using about 1 tablespoon of batter per pancake. Make sure you leave a small gap between the pancakes as they will spread slightly as they cook.

4. Cook the pancakes for 1–2 minutes, or until tiny bubbles start to appear on the surface, then carefully flip them using a fish slice or spatula and cook for a further 1–2 minutes. Repeat until all the batter is used (you may need to do this in batches, depending on the size of your pan).

5. Stack the pancakes on a plate, top with the icing sugar and maple syrup, then add the blueberries and serve.

Top Tip **If you need to cook the pancakes in batches, keep the cooked pancakes on a plate in the oven on a very low heat to keep them warm.**

HOMEMADE
HASH BROWNS

Making your own hash browns might sound complicated, but it's actually a lot easier than it looks. All you need is a large non-waxy potato, herbs and seasonings of your choice and some oil to fry the hash browns. That's it! The humble potato is transformed into crispy, crunchy bites of heaven in just a few steps. The hash browns can be served on their own (I like to dip them in sweet chilli sauce), as a side dish with poached, fried or scrambled eggs, or added to a full English breakfast.

Serves 1 (or can be served as a side dish for 2) | **Preparation time: 15–20 minutes**

1 large potato (about 220–240g), preferably a non-waxy variety, such as Maris Piper or King Edward

pinch each of salt and freshly ground black pepper

1 tsp dried rosemary

½ tbsp oil for frying, such as olive oil or cold-pressed rapeseed oil

½ tbsp chives, finely chopped (optional)

1. Give the potato a good scrub in cold water. I leave the skin on, but you can peel it if you prefer.

2. Grate the potato using a cheese grater, then place the grated potato in a clean cloth or tea towel. Squeeze the potato as hard as you can over the sink or a large bowl, until no more liquid comes out. Make sure not to skip this step, otherwise the hash browns will be soggy and less likely to bind together as a result.

3. Put the grated potato into a large mixing bowl and stir in the salt, pepper and rosemary.

4. Heat the oil in a large non-stick frying pan over a medium-high heat. Once the oil is hot, spoon the grated potato into the pan in 4 circular shapes. You can use greased egg or crumpet rings for neat hash browns or shape them freestyle if you prefer.

5. Cook the hash browns for 3–4 minutes, then carefully flip them over using a fish slice or spatula and cook for a further 3–4 minutes. At this point, they should be golden and crispy on the outside, but if they are looking pale, cook for a further minute on each side.

6. Transfer the hash browns to a plate, then sprinkle over the chopped chives, if using. Serve immediately.

Top Tip **Make the hash browns even tastier by stuffing them with a hidden cheese centre, which oozes as you slice into them. See page 109 for my Melt-in-the-middle Hash Browns recipe – it's definitely worth a try.**

PAN-FRIED
HALLOUMI

If you follow me on Instagram, you probably already know about my love affair with halloumi. This squeaky Cypriot cheese is a fantastic addition to breakfast and can be glazed with all sorts of herbs, spices and sauces before cooking. My trick for achieving grill lines on halloumi without digging out the griddle pan from the back of the cupboard, is simple: a crinkle knife. I bought one over five years ago to make homemade crinkle-cut chips and wondered if it would work on halloumi, so I gave it a go and have used it ever since. You can buy crinkle knives or cutters in kitchen shops or online; they are inexpensive and are fab for making homemade crinkle chips and vegetables too. I can't recommend them too highly!

Serves 1 | Preparation time: 10 minutes

30g halloumi cheese

1 heaped tsp sweet chilli sauce, for glazing (optional)

½ tsp oil for frying, such as olive oil or cold-pressed rapeseed oil

1. Slice the cheese into ½cm thick slices, using a crinkle knife if possible. If you like sweet chilli sauce, brush the slices all over with it, making sure they are evenly coated.

2. Heat the oil in a medium non-stick frying pan over a medium heat. Once the oil is hot, add the slices of halloumi.

3. Fry the halloumi on each side for 1–2 minutes. It may release some water as it cooks, but don't worry as this will evaporate. If you added sweet chilli sauce to the halloumi, keep a close eye on it while cooking and turn the heat down to low if it looks as though it is starting to burn.

4. Transfer the slices to a plate using a fish slice or spatula and serve immediately. One of my favourite ways to serve halloumi is on a crumpet with scrambled eggs. See page 14 for my Silky Scrambled Eggs recipe.

Top Tip Halloumi works really well with the sweet chilli sauce above, but you could also try swapping it for honey, maple syrup or even mango chutney instead. See page 90 for my Honey Balsamic-glazed Halloumi Crumpet recipe.

DUCKPOND

Duckpond is a name that has always been used by my family for egg-in-a-hole, which is a slice of fried bread with the centre cut out and an egg cooked in the middle. When my Mum and Aunt were children, you could guarantee that they would respond in unison with 'Duckpond!' when asked by my Nan what they'd like for breakfast. You can use something circular, such as the rim of a mug or an egg ring, to cut out the centre of the bread, but I also like to use different biscuit cutters, such as a star, heart or even a Christmas tree, for a fun twist. Oh, and don't forget to fry the cut-out centre too, as it's ideal for dipping into the yolk of the fried egg.

Serves 1 | Preparation time: 10 minutes

1 medium slice of white or wholemeal bread

½ tbsp oil for frying, such as olive oil or cold-pressed rapeseed oil

1 large free-range egg

pinch each of salt and freshly ground black pepper

1. Use an egg ring, mug rim or a biscuit cutter to cut a hole in the centre of the slice of bread.

2. Heat the oil in a large non-stick frying pan over a medium heat. Once the oil is hot, put the slice of bread and the cut-out centre in the pan.

3. Fry for 1–2 minutes, or until the bread starts to crisp up, then flip both pieces using a fish slice or spatula. Crack the egg into the centre of the bread, sprinkle over the salt and pepper, then turn the heat down to low.

4. Fry for 2–3 minutes, then check to see if the egg white is cooked to your liking. If not, continue to fry for a further minute. You can cover the pan with a lid to speed up the cooking time by steaming the top of the egg.

5. Once the white is cooked through, but the yolk still runny, carefully lift the Duckpond out of the pan and transfer it to a plate. Serve it with the cut-out centre alongside for dipping into the yolk.

Top Tip

Upgrade your Duckpond by swapping the toast for a giant crumpet or a bagel sliced in half (cut a slightly larger hole around each of the existing holes of the bagel and crack an egg into each bagel half).

Top Tip

For an easy upgrade, try stuffing the crumpets before soaking them in the whisked egg. All you need to do is cut a small circle in the centre of each crumpet and carefully scoop out the middle. Put a teaspoon of the filling of your choice in the hole, place the cut-out centre back (pressing down carefully) then continue with the remaining steps. You could add grated cheese for a savoury version or a teaspoon of Nutella, jam or Lotus Biscoff spread for a sweet one, and there's plenty of stuffed frumpet inspiration on my Instagram page if you get stuck for ideas!

FRUMPETS

At the beginning of 2016 I came up with the word 'frumpet' as an amusing, shortened name for French toast-style crumpets, which I frequently cook for breakfast. In fact, I have typed it so much over the past few years that the autocorrect on my phone now automatically changes the word crumpet to frumpet! The name seems to have caught on as I now see it being used regularly on Instagram, which never fails to make me smile! The beauty of the frumpet is that it works well in both sweet and savoury recipes, so I have included both below.

Serves 1 | Preparation time: 10 minutes

Basic frumpets

1 large free-range egg

2 crumpets

1 tsp oil for frying, such as olive oil, coconut oil or cold-pressed rapeseed oil

Savoury frumpets

pinch each of salt and freshly ground black pepper

1 tsp finely chopped herbs of your choice, such as rosemary or chives

20g finely grated cheese, such as mature or extra mature Cheddar (optional)

Sweet frumpets

½ tsp vanilla extract

1 tsp maple syrup, runny honey or icing sugar

80g sliced fruit or berries, such as banana, raspberries, blueberries or strawberries

1 tsp spread, such as Nutella or Lotus Biscoff spread

1. Crack the egg into a medium shallow bowl, then beat it with a fork or hand whisk until combined.

2. If you are making savoury frumpets, stir the salt, pepper, herbs and optional grated cheese into the whisked egg. If you are making sweet frumpets, stir the vanilla extract and maple syrup, honey or icing sugar into the whisked egg. Soak both crumpets in the egg mixture for 1 minute each side, making sure that they are well coated.

3. Heat the oil in a large non-stick frying pan over a medium heat. Once the oil is hot, fry the frumpets for 2–3 minutes on each side, or until they are golden brown and crispy.

4. Serve the savoury frumpets as they are and the sweet frumpets with the toppings of your choice.

SCRUMPETS

Scrumpets are another one of my breakfast inventions with an amusing made-up name. It describes my method of scrambling chopped up crumpets soaked in whisked egg in a frying pan until they are golden and crispy. Crumpets work particularly well for this because of their spongy texture, as the holes soak up the egg mixture easily. Scrumpets are incredibly versatile; you can add all sorts of ingredients for different flavour variations. I've added black pepper, chilli flakes and spring onion in this recipe, but why not try sprinkling over some crispy cooked bacon or chorizo once the scrumpets are cooked, or adding grated cheese with chopped chives to the egg mixture before frying? Get creative and find your own favourite scrumpet combination.

Serves 1 | **Preparation time: 10 minutes**

2 crumpets

1 large free-range egg

pinch each of salt and freshly ground black pepper, plus extra black pepper to garnish

½ tsp chilli flakes

1 tsp oil for frying, such as olive oil or cold-pressed rapeseed oil

1 spring onion, chopped into 1cm pieces (optional)

1. Chop the crumpets into small cubes, about 1.5–2cm in size. I use a pair of kitchen scissors, rather than a knife, for speed.

2. Crack the egg into a large mixing bowl, add the salt, pepper and chilli flakes, then beat them with a fork or hand whisk until everything is combined. Put the chopped crumpet pieces into the egg mixture, give them a good stir to ensure that they are evenly coated, then leave them to soak for 1–2 minutes.

3. While the crumpets are soaking, heat the oil in a large non-stick frying pan over a high heat. Once the pan is hot, tip in the scrumpet mixture. Cook over a medium-high heat, moving the scrumpets around the pan with a spatula or wooden spoon, so that they cook evenly, for 3–4 minutes, or until they are golden and crispy.

4. Transfer the scrumpets to a plate. Sprinkle over the chopped spring onion, if using, and an extra pinch of black pepper, then serve.

Top Tip   **You can speed things up even more by chopping the crumpets and spring onion the night before.**

BREAKFAST
TO GO

LEMON DRIZZLE
PORRIDGE MUFFINS

I recently had the idea of turning the breakfast staple of porridge into muffins which can be munched on the move. This turned out so well that I have been working my way through lots of different flavour combinations to find my favourite . . . any excuse to eat more of them! This is a zesty version, inspired by both the flavours and technique used in a lemon drizzle cake. You poke small holes in the muffins after baking them and pour over a sweet lemon drizzle, so the muffins soak it up. The muffins are denser than regular, cake-type muffins because of the high ratio of oats to flour, but you can switch the quantities of self-raising flour and oats to 100g each if you prefer a lighter texture.

Serves 6 | Preparation time: 25–30 minutes

butter or oil, for greasing

150g rolled oats

50g self-raising flour

½ tbsp runny honey

2 large free-range eggs

120ml semi-skimmed milk (or a non-dairy alternative)

zest of 1 large lemon, plus extra to garnish

For the drizzle

juice of 1 large lemon

1 tbsp granulated sugar

For the glaze (optional)

1 heaped tsp icing sugar

½ tsp cold water

1. Preheat your oven to 200°C/180°C fan/gas mark 6. Grease the 6 holes of a non-stick muffin tin with the butter or oil.

2. Combine the rolled oats and flour in a large mixing bowl. Add the honey, eggs, milk and lemon zest, then mix until combined.

3. Spoon the batter into the muffin tin, dividing it evenly between the holes.

4. Bake for 15 minutes, or until the muffins are golden. To check if the muffins are ready, insert a skewer into the centre of one – it should come out clean, but if not bake for a further 5 minutes.

5. While the muffins are in the oven, prepare the drizzle by mixing the lemon juice and sugar in a small bowl. As soon as the muffins are ready and while they are still in the tin, poke lots of small holes in the top of each muffin using a skewer or toothpick, then spoon over the drizzle. Leave the muffins to absorb the drizzle for a few minutes, then carefully remove them from the tin and transfer them to a plate.

6. For the glaze, put the icing sugar into a small bowl. Gradually add the cold water a few drops at a time, until you have a runny consistency, then drizzle this over the top of the muffins. Grate over some additional lemon zest if desired.

7. Either serve the muffins while they are still warm or leave them to cool completely before storing them in an airtight container in the fridge for up to 3 days.

Top Tip

Add ½ tablespoon poppy seeds to the mixture for a lemon and poppy seed version.

SMOKED SALMON *and*
CREAM CHEESE TOAST QUICHE

This is the classic breakfast combination of smoked salmon and eggs on toast, but not as you know it! This was the first recipe I came up with when writing this book. I wanted to create a quiche-like bake, using bread instead of pastry for the casing, to give it a breakfast theme, and I think it works really well. The buttered bread transforms into crispy toast in the oven, providing a superb contrast in texture to the soft filling. Another breakfast that you can prepare ahead of time, this keeps well in the fridge for up to three days and is gorgeous served either hot or cold. Just grab a slice and go!

Serves 6 | Preparation time: 45–50 minutes

8 medium slices of white or wholemeal bread, crusts cut off

100g softened salted butter, plus extra for greasing

6 large free-range eggs

150g smoked salmon, roughly chopped

100g cream cheese

zest and juice of ½ lemon, plus extra to garnish

½ tbsp chives, finely chopped

½ tsp dried tarragon

pinch each of salt and freshly ground black pepper

1. Preheat your oven to 200°C/180°C fan/gas mark 6, then grease a 20cm non-stick springform cake tin.

2. Spread each slice of bread with the butter on both sides, then cut the slices in half.

3. Arrange the slices of bread to form a case in the cake tin, pressing them into the base and sides and overlapping them to ensure that there are no gaps.

4. Bake for 10 minutes, or until the toast is starting to turn golden and crispy. Fill any gaps that have formed where the bread shrinks slightly as it cooks by pressing the leftover crusts into the tin.

5. Meanwhile, crack the eggs into a large mixing bowl, then beat them with a fork or hand whisk until combined. Add the smoked salmon, cream cheese, lemon zest and juice, chives, tarragon and salt and pepper, then mix well.

6. Pour the egg mixture into the toast crust, then carefully place the tin back in the oven and bake for a further 25–30 minutes, or until the egg has set. Check whether the eggs are cooked by inserting a skewer into the centre; it should come out clean.

7. Remove the tin from the oven, then leave it to cool slightly before opening the latch of the springform tin to release the sides. Carefully lift the toast quiche from the base and place it on a plate, then serve immediately. Alternatively, allow the quiche to cool completely on a wire rack before transferring it to an airtight container to store in the fridge for up to 3 days.

Top Tip

Not a fish lover? Try switching the smoked salmon, cream cheese, lemon and herbs for 150g cooked and roughly-chopped smoked bacon, 100g grated mature or extra mature Cheddar cheese, 1 heaped tablespoon of crème fraîche and 1 teaspoon of dried thyme. Or for a veggie version, add 150g wilted baby spinach, 100g grated Gruyère cheese, 50ml double cream and ¼ teaspoon of ground nutmeg.

JAM DOUGHNUT
SCRUMPET BITES

A doughnut for breakfast isn't the healthiest of options, so I have transformed my scrumpet (scrambled crumpet, see page 34) recipe into delicious oven-baked bites with a jam doughnut theme. They have a strawberry jam centre that oozes as you sink your teeth into them and are rolled in granulated sugar while still warm, to replicate the flavours and texture of a filled doughnut. Yum!

Serves 6 | Preparation time: 25–30 minutes

oil or butter, for greasing

4 crumpets

2 large free-range eggs

40ml semi-skimmed milk
(or a non-dairy alternative)

½ tsp vanilla extract

6 tsp strawberry jam (or other jam
of your choice)

1 tbsp granulated sugar

1. Preheat your oven to 200°C/180°C fan/gas mark 6. Grease the 6 holes of a non-stick muffin tin with the oil or butter.

2. Using a pair of kitchen scissors, chop the crumpets into small pieces about 1.5cm–2cm in size, then set them aside.

3. Crack the eggs into a large mixing bowl, then beat them with the milk and vanilla extract using a fork or hand whisk. Add the chopped crumpets to the bowl, give the mixture a good stir to make sure everything is combined, then leave to sit for a few minutes so the crumpets absorb the egg mixture.

4. Spoon half the scrumpet mixture into the muffin tin, dividing it evenly between the 6 holes. Put a teaspoon of jam in the centre of each muffin, then spoon over the remaining mixture, making sure that the jam is completely covered.

5. Bake for 15–20 minutes, or until they are golden brown.

6. Put the granulated sugar on a small plate. Allow the scrumpet bites to cool slightly for a few minutes before carefully removing them from the muffin tin, then roll them in the sugar, making sure that all sides are coated. Either serve them immediately while still warm, or allow them to cool completely on a wire rack before storing them in the fridge in an airtight container for up to 3 days.

Top Tip

For a low-sugar version, use a low-sugar jam and swap the sugar for sweetener.

OMELETTE LOAF

I first came up with the idea of a baked omelette loaf in 2018, as a breakfast you can bake in advance, keep in the fridge and slice as required (you can eat it cold or reheat it in the microwave). The loaf is packed with protein from the eggs, which makes it really filling, and it's so tasty that I still regularly prepare it for quick weekday breakfasts, lunches and even as part of a picnic. What I love about this recipe is that it's a fantastic way to use up any odds and ends in your fridge. Got some cooked ham that you don't know how to use? Throw it in the loaf! I've tried adding different scraps of vegetables, cheese and cooked meat over the years, ranging from chorizo, chilli and grated halloumi to pesto, mozzarella and cherry tomatoes, and it always turns out absolutely yummy, so don't be afraid to experiment with different flavours.

Serves 6 | **Preparation time: 45 minutes**

½ tsp oil for frying, such as olive oil or cold-pressed rapeseed oil, plus extra for greasing

2 leeks

150g baby spinach

1 clove garlic, crushed

6 large free-range eggs

pinch each of salt and freshly ground black pepper

½ tsp dried rosemary

½ tsp dried thyme

150g mature or extra mature Cheddar (or other cheese of your choice), grated

1. Preheat your oven to 200°C/180°C fan/gas mark 6, then grease a 900g non-stick loaf tin with the oil or butter.

2. Trim the leeks, cut each in half vertically from top to bottom, then slice them across into 2cm pieces.

3. Heat the oil in a large non-stick frying pan over a medium heat. Once the oil is hot, add the leeks and cook them for 5 minutes, or until softened, stirring regularly to make sure that they don't catch.

4. Add the baby spinach to the pan, cook for about 2 minutes, or until the spinach has wilted, then add the crushed garlic and cook for a further minute.

5. Meanwhile, crack the eggs into a large mixing bowl, then beat them with a fork or hand whisk until combined. Stir in the salt, pepper, rosemary, thyme and most of the Cheddar, saving a handful to top the loaf.

6. Once the vegetables are cooked, tip them into the mixing bowl and give the mixture a good stir to make sure everything is well combined. Pour the omelette mixture into the loaf tin, then top with the remaining Cheddar.

7. Bake for 30–35 minutes, or until the loaf is golden brown and risen. You can check if it is cooked by inserting a skewer into the middle, which should come out clean.

8. Leave the loaf to cool slightly before carefully removing it from the tin. Either serve it immediately or leave it to cool completely on a wire rack, before storing it in an airtight container in the fridge. The loaf can be kept in the fridge for upto 3 days and can also be frozen for up to 3 months. I recommend slicing the loaf into portions before freezing and storing the slices individually with a piece of greaseproof paper between each slice to prevent them becoming stuck together.

Top Tip

Try my filo version (also known as a fi-loaf!), which is the same recipe with the addition of a flaky, filo pastry crust. All you need to do is grease your loaf tin, then slice 3 sheets of ready-made filo pastry in half and use them to line the tin, overlapping them and making sure there are no gaps. Brush the filo pastry all over with 10g melted butter, then bake it for 5 minutes before pouring in the omelette mixture and following the remaining steps in the recipe above.

BAKE-AHEAD
FRUITY MUESLI CUPS

A different way to enjoy your morning muesli, these yummy baked cups can be prepared the night before and the fillings added the next morning for a speedy brekkie. I have suggested three different fillings, so you can mix and match or pick your favourite, but feel free to make up your own combinations too. Try baking the cups on a Sunday so that you can have a lie-in for a few days at the beginning of the week, knowing that breakfast is already made!

Serves 6 | Preparation time: 15 minutes, plus 5 minutes to prepare the fillings the next morning

½ tbsp melted coconut oil or unsalted butter, plus extra for greasing

1 large ripe banana

100g fruit-flavoured muesli of your choice

25g rolled oats

Top Tip

Stir an additional teaspoon of cocoa powder and a teaspoon of runny honey into the muesli mixture for a chocolate version.

Filling options (for 6 cups)

★ 50g Greek yoghurt, 40g blueberries and 3 large strawberries, hulled and sliced

★ 6 tsp smooth or crunchy peanut butter (1 tsp per cup), 6 tsp strawberry jam (1 tsp per cup) and 3 large strawberries, hulled and sliced

★ 150g cream cheese mixed with ½ tbsp runny honey and 40g roughly mashed blueberries, plus a few whole blueberries to top each cup

1. Preheat your oven to 200°C/180°C fan/gas mark 6. Grease the 6 holes of a non-stick muffin tin with the coconut oil or butter.

2. Peel then roughly mash the banana with a fork in a large

mixing bowl. Add the muesli, oats and coconut oil or butter, then stir until combined.

3. Spoon the muesli mixture into the muffin tin, dividing it evenly between the holes. Shape the mixture into cups by pressing it into the base and sides of each muffin hole, leaving a space in the centre to add the fillings after baking.

4. Bake for 10 minutes, or until the cups are golden brown and firm. Carefully remove them from the muffin tin, then leave them to cool completely on a wire rack before transferring them to an airtight container.

5. The next morning, prepare your choice of fillings, then spoon it into the cups. Serve immediately.

Top Tip — **Not a fan of baked beans? Swap the beans for two heaped tablespoons of green or red pesto or caramelised red onion chutney.**

CHEESY BAKED BEAN
CRUFFINS

A hybrid of a croissant and a muffin, a cruffin is a sweet pastry you usually find in upmarket coffee shops and bakeries, which has become a trend in recent years. This is my super simple cruffin recipe with a savoury twist, filled with the ultimate comfort food: baked beans and melted cheese. The cruffins are really quick and easy to prepare using ready-made croissant dough, which you can find in the fridge section with other ready-made pastry in most major supermarkets. Or if you have the skills, by all means make your own croissant dough!

Serves 6 (makes 12 cruffins) | **Preparation time: 20 minutes**

plain flour, for dusting

butter or oil, for greasing

1 pack (350g) ready-rolled croissant dough

1 large tin (415g) baked beans

150g mature or extra mature Cheddar, grated

1 tsp chilli flakes (optional)

1. Preheat your oven to 200°C/180°C fan/gas mark 6. Grease a 12-hole muffin tin with the butter or oil.

2. Unroll the croissant dough on a large floured chopping board. Ignore the pre-cut diagonal lines and slice along each horizontal line with a knife to create 3 rectangles of dough.

3. Spoon the baked beans on to the croissant dough, distributing them evenly inside each rectangle of dough and leaving a small border around the edges. Sprinkle the Cheddar on top of the beans, again distributing it evenly between the rectangles.

4. Roll up each rectangle from the short edge (as if you were making a Swiss roll), then slice each roll into 4 evenly sized pieces. Carefully place the croissant swirls in the muffin tin with the fillings facing up.

5. Bake for 15 minutes, or until they are golden brown. Leave them to cool slightly before removing them from the tin. Transfer them to a plate and sprinkle them with the chilli flakes, if desired, before serving. The cruffins can be served hot or cold and reheated if required.

MELT-IN-THE-MIDDLE
CHOCOLATE CHIP
BRIOCHE MUFFINS

These melt-in-the-middle muffins with a gooey Nutella centre are a wonderful way to use the chocolate chip brioche rolls you can find in most supermarkets. These muffins are sure to be a hit with adults and children alike, and will keep in the fridge for three days. They can be frozen for up to three months, making them ideal for baking ahead of time. Delicious served warm or cold, they are great for taking with you on the go . . . if you can resist eating them straight from the oven!

Serves 12 | Preparation time: 30 minutes

oil or butter, for greasing

8 chocolate chip brioche rolls

3 large free-range eggs

100ml semi-skimmed milk
(or a non-dairy alternative)

1 tsp vanilla extract

6 tsp Nutella (or an alternative
chocolate spread)

20g milk chocolate chips
(optional)

1. Preheat your oven to 200°C/180°C fan/gas mark 6. Grease a non-stick 12-hole muffin tin with the oil or butter.

2. Roughly tear or slice the brioche rolls into small pieces about 2cm in size.

3. Crack the eggs into a large mixing bowl, then beat them with the milk and vanilla extract, using a fork or hand whisk. Add the torn brioche pieces to the bowl, give the mixture a good stir to make sure everything is combined, then leave it to sit for a few minutes so the brioche pieces absorb the egg mixture.

4. Spoon half the mixture into the muffin tin, dividing it evenly between the 12 holes. Put half a teaspoon of Nutella in the centre of each muffin, then spoon over the remaining mixture, making sure the Nutella is completely covered. Sprinkle the chocolate chips over the top of the muffins, if using.

5. Bake for 20 minutes, or until they are golden brown. Leave them to cool slightly before carefully removing them from the tin and transferring them to a plate. Either serve them immediately while still warm or allow them to cool completely on a wire rack before storing them in the fridge in an airtight container for up to 3 days.

HONEY MUSTARD SAUSAGE
and EGG BITES

This may not be the prettiest breakfast, but these sausage and egg bites certainly pack a punch when it comes to taste. The inspiration behind this recipe is my Mum, who is a fantastic cook. Ever since I was little, she has baked cocktail sausages glazed with honey and wholegrain mustard for family parties or celebrations. They are so good that I have usually devoured most of them only a few minutes after the party has begun, so she now buys extra sausages to cook to make up for my gluttony (sorry, Mum)! The combination of sweet honey, tangy wholegrain mustard and pork sausages is out of this world, although you can leave out the honey and mustard if you wish, as the bites are still delightful without them. Just try not to scoff them all in one go like I could . . .

Serves 6 | Preparation time: 35–40 minutes

butter or oil, for greasing

6 good-quality pork sausages

½ tbsp runny honey

½ tbsp wholegrain mustard

3 large free-range eggs

pinch each of salt and freshly ground black pepper

½ tsp dried or fresh chopped thyme

¼ tsp dried or fresh chopped rosemary

1. Preheat your oven to 200°C/180°C fan/gas mark 6. Grease the 6 holes of a non-stick muffin tin with the butter or oil.

2. Cut the links between the sausages using a pair of kitchen scissors. Squeeze the meat out of the casing of each sausage into a large mixing bowl and discard the casing. Add the honey and mustard to the bowl, then mix well so they are well combined with the sausagemeat.

3. Divide the mixture between the holes of the muffin tin, then shape it into cups by pressing it into the base and sides of each hole, leaving a space in the centre for the egg mixture.

4. Crack the eggs into a large jug, add the salt, pepper, thyme and rosemary, then whisk until everything is combined. Pour the egg mixture into the centre of each cup, leaving a small gap at the top so that they do not overflow.

5. Bake for 30 minutes, or until the eggs are set and the sausage meat is completely cooked. You can check if the eggs are cooked by inserting a skewer into the centre, which should come out clean.

6. Carefully remove the bites from the tin and serve immediately. Alternatively, allow them to cool completely on a wire rack before transferring to an airtight container to store in the fridge for up to 3 days.

Top Tip

Swap plain pork sausages for flavoured sausages, such as pork and leek, or pork and apple (and leave out the honey and mustard, if you like). You could also use chicken or vegetarian sausages.

ETON MESS
OVERNIGHT OATS

Inspired by the iconic English summer dessert Eton Mess, this is a simply lovely breakfast to take with you on a warm sunny day. It really makes the most of plump juicy strawberries while they are in season, which add a natural sweetness to the oats, and the meringue crumbled on top provides an (optional) indulgent twist. Don't forget to take a spoon with you if you take it as a breakfast to go!

Serves 1 | Preparation time: 10 minutes, plus 8 hours soaking overnight

80g strawberries, hulled and chopped into quarters

40g rolled oats

100ml semi-skimmed milk (or a non-dairy alternative)

1 tsp runny honey

80g natural or Greek yoghurt

½ meringue nest (optional)

1. Roughly mash half the strawberries in a medium shallow bowl. Add the oats, milk and honey, give them a good stir, then cover the bowl and place it in the fridge, ideally overnight, but for at least an hour to give the oats plenty of time to absorb the liquid.

2. The next morning, assemble the oats in a container or jar, layering them with the yoghurt and the remaining chopped strawberries. It doesn't have to be particularly neat; this is Eton mess-style!

3. Crumble over half a meringue nest, if using, immediately before eating, then serve.

Top Tip
Try swapping the strawberries for fresh raspberries instead.

SCRAMBLED
NAAN MUFFINS

Leftover naan bread is usually unheard of in my house, but these muffins are a
brilliant way to use up excess naan before it goes stale. Whether you prefer to make
your own, buy packs from the supermarket, or order it as part of a takeaway, any
variety of naan bread will work. Try plain, garlic and coriander or even my favourite,
Peshwari naan, which gives the muffins a gorgeous coconut flavour.

Serves 8 | Preparation time: 35 minutes

½ tsp oil for frying, such as olive, coconut or rapeseed oil, plus extra for greasing

1 medium red onion (about 75g), diced

½ tsp ground cumin

½ tsp garam masala

¼ tsp ground coriander

¼ tsp ground turmeric

½ tsp nigella (black onion) seeds

1 clove garlic, crushed

100g cherry tomatoes, cut into quarters

2 large free-range eggs

100ml semi-skimmed milk (or a non-dairy alternative)

pinch each of salt and freshly ground black pepper

2 large naan breads (about 250g), any flavour

1 tsp chilli flakes (optional)

1. Preheat your oven to 200°C/180°C fan/gas mark 6. Grease the 8 holes of a non-stick muffin tin with the oil or butter.

2. Heat the oil in a large non-stick frying pan over a medium heat. Once the oil is hot, add the red onion and fry for 3–4 minutes, or until it is soft and translucent. Add the cumin, garam masala, coriander, turmeric, nigella seeds and garlic to the pan and cook for a further minute. Add the quartered cherry tomatoes and cook for 2 minutes, then remove the pan from the heat.

3. Crack the eggs into a large mixing bowl and beat them with the milk and salt and pepper, using a fork or hand whisk. Tip the spiced onion and tomatoes into the bowl and mix well.

4. Roughly tear or slice the naan bread into small pieces about 2cm in size. Add the pieces to the bowl and give the mixture a good stir to make sure everything is combined, then leave the pieces to soak for a few minutes so that they absorb the spiced egg mixture.

5. Spoon the mixture into the muffin tin, dividing it evenly between the holes. Sprinkle the chilli flakes over the top of the muffins, if using.

6. Bake for 20 minutes, or until the muffins are golden brown. Leave them to cool slightly before carefully removing them from the tin and transferring them to a plate. Either serve them immediately while they are still warm or allow them to cool completely on a wire rack before storing them in the fridge in an airtight container for up to 3 days.

Top Tip If you don't have all the spices to hand, use
½ tablespoon of mild curry powder.

Top Tip

Swap the cornflakes and Cheerios for another cereal such as Rice Krispies, Coco Pops or granola.

HONEY NUT
CEREAL BARS

You are guaranteed to make your colleagues envious if you bring these honey nut cereal bars to the office for your breakfast. Or if you're feeling generous you can share them, as the recipe makes 12 bars. Ideal to grab before leaving the house, the bars make excellent snacks and lunchbox fillers too. My recipe includes peanut butter, but you could swap it for another nut butter, such as almond butter, if you prefer. The bars will keep in an airtight container in the fridge for up to a week, although you'll probably want to eat them all sooner!

Serves 12 | Preparation time: 15 minutes, plus at least 40 minutes to set

125g peanut butter, crunchy or smooth

125g runny honey

pinch of sea salt flakes

50g cornflakes

50g Cheerios

45g unsalted nuts, roughly chopped (I use a mix of pecans, walnuts and cashews)

1. Line a 20 x 20cm baking tin with baking paper.

2. In a large saucepan, heat the peanut butter, honey and sea salt over a low heat, stirring regularly with a wooden spoon, until the mixture begins to bubble.

3. Remove the pan from the heat then add the cereal and chopped nuts to the saucepan and mix well, ensuring that the cereal and nuts are evenly coated with the honey and peanut butter mixture.

4. Spoon the mixture into the baking tin in an even layer, then press it down gently with the back of the spoon, being careful not to break the cereal pieces. Sprinkle an extra pinch of sea salt over the top, if you like.

5. Leave the mixture to cool for 10 minutes before transferring the tin to the fridge and allowing it to set for at least 30 minutes. You can speed up the setting time by putting the tin in the freezer for 15 minutes before transferring it to the fridge.

6. Once the mixture has set, carefully remove it from the tin and place it on a chopping board, then slice it into 12 bars (or squares) using a large knife. Either serve the bars immediately or store them in an airtight container in the fridge for up to a week.

MEXICAN-STYLE
TORTILLA EGG CUPS

I have taken a baked egg muffin to the next level by adding fajita-style flavours and crispy tortilla shells. Yummy for breakfast, as well as lunch or a light dinner, these cups are guaranteed to disappear in no time!

Serves 12 | Preparation time: 20–25 minutes

butter or oil, for greasing

3 large wheat tortilla wraps

4 large free-range eggs

1 tbsp sour cream

1 large or 2 small red or yellow peppers, cored and diced

2 spring onions, finely chopped

60g mozzarella cheese, grated

1 tsp smoked paprika

½ tsp ground cumin

¼ tsp garlic granules

½ tsp dried oregano

pinch of salt and freshly ground black pepper

½ tsp chilli flakes (optional)

1. Preheat your oven to 200°C/180°C fan/gas mark 6. Grease a 12-hole muffin tin with the butter or oil.

2. Place a tortilla wrap on a chopping board, then cut small circles in the wrap with a knife, using a ramekin, the rim of a mug or an egg ring as a template. You should be able to get at least 4 small circles out of each wrap. Repeat with the remaining wraps.

3. Press a tortilla circle into each hole of the muffin tin.

4. Crack the eggs into a large mixing bowl, then beat them with a fork or hand whisk. Add the sour cream, pepper, spring onion, mozzarella, smoked paprika, cumin, garlic, oregano, salt and pepper, then mix well.

5. Pour the egg mixture into the tortilla cups, distributing it evenly. Sprinkle over the chilli flakes, if using.

6. Bake for 15 minutes, or until the eggs are set. You can check whether the eggs are cooked by inserting a skewer into the centre of a cup; it should come out clean.

7. Carefully remove the cups from the muffin tin and transfer them to a plate, then serve immediately. Alternatively, allow them to cool completely on a wire rack before transferring them to an airtight container to store in the fridge for up to 3 days.

Top Tip

Don't throw away the leftover pieces of the tortilla wraps; use them to make homemade tortilla crisps! Cut them into triangles, season with salt (or half a teaspoon of fajita seasoning), pour a drizzle of oil over the top, then arrange them in a single layer on a baking tray and bake at 200°C/180°C fan/gas mark 6 for 8 minutes.

BLUEBERRY *and* LEMON
MUESLI LOAF

This muesli loaf is absolutely divine served warm from the oven, accompanied by a steaming cup of tea or coffee. I like to top slices with blueberry jam, but other toppings, such as nut butter or yoghurt with set honey, are also favourites.

Serves 6 | **Preparation time: 45–50 minutes**

oil or butter, for greasing

150g muesli of your choice, plus extra for topping

150g self-raising flour

zest and juice of ½ large lemon

2 large free-range eggs

200ml semi-skimmed milk (or a non-dairy alternative)

3 tbsp runny honey

120g blueberries

1. Preheat your oven to 200°C/180°C fan/gas mark 6 then grease a 900g non-stick loaf tin.

2. Put the muesli, flour and lemon zest into a large mixing bowl and give them a quick stir. Add the lemon juice, eggs, milk and honey, and mix until everything is well combined.

3. Spoon enough batter into the loaf tin to cover the base (this prevents the blueberries sinking to the bottom of the loaf). Stir the blueberries into the remaining batter, then pour it into the loaf tin.

4. Top the batter with an extra handful of muesli if desired, then bake the loaf for 35–40 minutes, or until a skewer inserted into the centre of the loaf comes out clean.

5. Leave the loaf to cool slightly before carefully removing it from the tin. Either serve it immediately (it is best enjoyed warm, but can be served cold) or leave it to cool completely on a wire rack before storing it in an airtight container.

HARISSA BAKED BEAN *and* CHORIZO
PUFF PASTRY MELTS

I have spiced up this classic sausage and bean melt by adding harissa paste to the beans and swapping the sausages for chorizo. This combination is sure to rouse your taste buds without being overwhelmingly hot. Use ready-rolled puff pastry to make these melts quick and easy to assemble.

Serves 4 | Preparation time: 25–30 minutes

plain flour, for dusting

1 sheet (320g) ready-rolled puff pastry

1 large tin (415g) baked beans

1 tsp harissa paste

80g chorizo, diced

100g mature or extra-mature Cheddar, grated

1 large free-range egg, beaten

1. Preheat your oven to 200°C/180°C fan/gas mark 6. Line a large baking tray with baking paper.

2. Unroll the sheet of ready-made puff pastry on a lightly floured surface or large chopping board. Slice the pastry in half vertically, then slice each half again so you have 4 rectangles of pastry.

3. In a medium-sized bowl, mix the baked beans with the harissa paste and chorizo. Put a large spoonful of the baked bean mixture on the top half of each pastry rectangle, dividing the mixture evenly between each and leaving a 1cm border around the edges. Top the beans with the grated Cheddar, again dividing it evenly.

4. Brush the borders of the pastry with the beaten egg, then gently fold over the remaining half of the pastry so the fillings are completely covered. Press firmly around the edges to ensure that the filling doesn't leak out. Crimp the edges of the pastries with a fork, then brush them all over with the egg. Use a sharp knife to make a few slits in the top of each one to allow steam to escape during cooking.

5. Bake the pastries for 15–20 minutes, or until they are puffed up and golden brown. Leave them to cool slightly and either serve them immediately or allow them to cool completely on a wire rack before transferring them to an airtight container and storing them in the fridge. They will keep in the fridge for 3 days and can be frozen for up to 3 months. If you freeze the pastries make sure you thaw them fully and reheat in the oven until the centres are piping hot.

Top Tip

Leave out the chorizo for a vegetarian-friendly version.

Top Tip

Don't throw away the crusts! You can use them to make croutons for other recipes or if you have any egg mixture left over, rustle up some French toast croutons for a quick breakfast. Cut the crusts into 1cm cubes, soak them in the remaining egg mixture, then heat a medium non-stick frying pan with half a teaspoon of oil over a medium heat. Once the oil is hot, add the croutons and fry them for 2–3 minutes, moving them around the pan so they cook evenly on all sides, then serve. They are scrumptious drizzled with maple syrup and served with fresh fruit such as banana slices or blueberries.

BISCOFF *and* BANANA
FRENCH TOAST CUPS

French toast in a portable cup form! Have you ever fancied French toast for breakfast, but needed to dash out of the door? Well, now you can take it out and about, with no cutlery required! I have put Lotus Biscoff spread and banana slices in the centre of each cup, as they are a marvellous combination, but you could swap the Biscoff spread for Nutella or peanut butter, or the banana for another fruit such as raspberries or blueberries. The flavour possibilities are endless!

Serves 6 | Preparation time: 20–25 minutes

oil or butter, for greasing

6 medium slices of white or wholemeal bread

2 large free-range eggs

20ml semi-skimmed milk (or a non-dairy alternative)

1 tsp vanilla extract

½ tsp ground cinnamon

½ tbsp maple syrup

For the filling

1 large banana, sliced into ½cm coins

3 tsp Lotus Biscoff spread

1. Preheat your oven to 200°C/180°C fan/gas mark 6. Grease the 6 holes of a non-stick muffin tin with the oil or butter.

2. Cut the crusts off the slices of bread, then set the slices aside.

3. Crack the eggs into a medium-sized shallow bowl, then beat in the milk, vanilla extract, cinnamon and maple syrup using a fork or hand whisk.

4. Soak both sides of a slice of bread in the egg mixture, allow any excess to run off, then press the slice into the muffin tin to create a cup shape. Repeat with the other 5 slices of bread.

5. Bake the cups for 15 minutes, or until they are crispy and golden brown. Leave the cups to cool slightly before carefully removing them from the tin and transferring them to a plate. Either add the fillings and serve the cups while they are still warm, or allow them to cool completely on a wire rack, before storing them in the fridge in an airtight container for up to 3 days (add the filling just before serving).

EVERYDAY
BREAKFASTS

EGG IN AN
ENGLISH MUFFIN BASKET

Simple and quick to prepare, this egg in an English muffin is similar to my recipe for Duckpond (see page 30), but uses a baked English muffin rather than fried bread to hold the egg. This is a fantastic basic recipe that you can enjoy as it is, or add various other ingredients before the egg. Try adding a slice of smoked salmon and half a tablespoon of crème fraîche before the egg, or 30g grated mature Cheddar and a chopped slice of ham. Have fun experimenting!

Serves 1 | Preparation time: 10–15 minutes

1 English muffin

10g melted butter

1 large free-range egg

pinch each of salt and freshly ground black pepper

pinch of chilli flakes and ½ tbsp chives, finely chopped (optional)

1. Preheat your oven to 200°C/180°C fan/gas mark 6. Line a baking tray with baking paper.

2. Use a sharp knife to cut a circle in the centre of the muffin, leaving a 1cm border around the edges. Scoop out the centre of the muffin, then set it aside. Press your fingers lightly against the base and walls of the muffin to create a defined well. Make sure you keep them intact so the fillings do not leak out.

3. Place the muffin and the cut-out centre on the baking tray, then brush the top and sides of both with the melted butter.

4. Separate the egg, setting the yolk aside, then put the egg white in the centre of the muffin. Season with the salt and pepper.

5. Bake for 7–8 minutes, or until the egg white has set, then add the egg yolk to the centre and bake for a further 2–3 minutes, so the yolk is still runny.

6. Transfer the muffin to a plate using a fish slice or spatula and garnish with the chilli flakes and chopped chives, if using, then serve. Don't forget to dip the crispy cut-out muffin centre into the yolk!

Top Tip The recipe serves one, but can easily be scaled up to serve more.

CHERRY BAKEWELL
CHEESECAKE BAGEL

I have taken the classic bagel topped with cream cheese to a whole new level with a quick-to-prepare fruity bagel topping that combines the flavours of two desserts, Bakewell tart and cheesecake, in one. The stars of the recipe are definitely the almond extract and the cherries, so don't miss them out!

Serves 1 | Preparation time: 10 minutes

1 plain bagel

25g cream cheese

¼ tsp almond extract

½ tsp runny honey

1 tsp black cherry jam

80g cherries, pitted and halved

20g flaked almonds

1. Slice the bagel in half, then toast it to your liking.

2. While the bagel is toasting, mix the cream cheese with the almond extract and honey. Transfer the bagel to a plate, spread both halves with the cream cheese mixture, then swirl through the jam.

3. Top the bagel halves with the cherries and flaked almonds, then serve.

Top Tip

Try this combination on toast or a toasted crumpet instead.

CAPRESE
HASSELBACK CROISSANT

True story: last February, in the middle of the night, I suddenly sat up in bed and announced 'Hasselback crumpets!' before making a note on my phone and going back to sleep. A strange moment, but my sleepy brain was clearly on to something and the next morning I tried making Hasselback crumpets, stuffing them with cheese and Marmite. They were a great success. The technique is usually reserved for potatoes: you slice them with a sharp knife, which gives them a bigger surface area and offers the opportunity to infuse them with flavour. Shortly after my Hasselback crumpet discovery, I found that a Hasselback croissant works brilliantly too, as you can stuff the gaps with all kinds of ingredients. This recipe is by no means an authentic Italian dish, but I have taken the main ingredients from an Italian Caprese salad and combined them with a classic French croissant to make a scrumptious amalgamation. The recipe serves one, but it's easy to increase the quantities if you have lots of hungry mouths to feed!

Serves 1 | Preparation time: 10–15 minutes

1 croissant

1 salad tomato, sliced

25g mozzarella, sliced

4 or 5 fresh basil leaves

1 tsp extra virgin olive oil

pinch each of salt and freshly ground black pepper

1. Preheat your oven to 200°C/180°C fan/gas mark 6.

2. Use a sharp knife to make 7 or 8 cuts along the croissant, being careful not to slice all the way through.

3. Place the croissant on a baking tray, then stuff the gaps with the sliced tomato, mozzarella and basil leaves.

4. Drizzle over the olive oil and add the salt and pepper, then bake for 5–10 minutes, or until the croissant is golden and crispy and the mozzarella is gooey.

5. Transfer the croissant to a plate using a fish slice or spatula and serve immediately.

Top Tip

When serving, drizzle the croissant with some balsamic vinegar or glaze to really make the flavours sing!

CORNFLAKE TART
BREAKFAST PARFAIT

A school dinner classic, cornflake tart is one of my all-time favourite desserts, as the crunchy, syrupy cornflakes and fruity strawberry jam work stunningly well together. As cornflakes and jam are breakfast (and cupboard) staples, I have combined honey nut cornflakes with strawberry jam and fresh strawberries in this breakfast parfait. Adding Greek yoghurt balances the sweetness. This is incredibly easy and quick to assemble, so you'll definitely want to include it in your weekday breakfast repertoire.

Serves 1 | Preparation time: 5 minutes

30g honey nut cornflakes

40g strawberries, hulled and chopped into quarters

½ tbsp strawberry jam

80g Greek yoghurt

1. Assemble the ingredients in a jar or glass, layering the cornflakes with the chopped strawberries, strawberry jam and yoghurt, then serve. Easy!

Top Tip

If honey nut cornflakes are too sweet for you, use plain cornflakes instead.

PESTO
COURGETTE HASH

We all know that pesto is the best-o! This one-pan breakfast is healthy, easy to prepare and can be served for lunch or dinner too. You can either enjoy it as it is, or serve it with some crusty bread or toast to dip into the yolks. Even less washing up is required if you eat it straight from the pan!

Serves 1 | Preparation time: 10–15 minutes

1 medium courgette

½ tsp oil for frying, such as olive oil or cold-pressed rapeseed oil

1 heaped tsp green pesto

2 large free-range eggs

pinch each of salt and freshly ground black pepper

15g Pecorino Romano cheese, finely grated (optional)

pinch of chilli flakes and a few torn basil leaves, to garnish (optional)

1. Remove the top and end of the courgette, then spiralise it.

2. Heat the oil in a medium non-stick frying pan over a medium heat. Once the oil is hot, add the spiralised courgette and the pesto, giving them a good stir to ensure that the pesto coats the courgette. Cook for 1–2 minutes until the courgette is slightly softened.

3. Create two small wells in the centre of the courgette, then crack the eggs into the gaps. Cook for a further 3–4 minutes, or until the egg whites have set, but the yolks remain runny. You can also cover the pan with a lid, which will speed up the cooking time by steaming the top of the eggs.

4. Carefully transfer the hash on to a large plate, then add the salt and pepper. Grate over the cheese, then garnish with a pinch of chilli flakes and a few torn basil leaves if desired. Serve immediately.

Top Tip

If you don't have a spiraliser, you can make courgetti using a vegetable peeler. Hold the courgette vertically and peel downwards (being careful of your fingers) to create long, thin ribbons.

BANOFFEE
PORRIDGE

I have replicated the flavours of the much-loved banoffee pie in this decadent bowl of porridge by topping it with toffee sauce, caramelised banana and grated dark chocolate. It is worth following the extra step of caramelising the banana, which really emphasises the toffee flavours!

Serves 1 | Preparation time: 10 minutes

1 large ripe banana

40g rolled oats

125ml cold water

100ml semi-skimmed milk
(or a non-dairy alternative)

½ tsp oil for frying, such as
coconut oil or cold-pressed
rapeseed oil

15g toffee sauce

½ square of dark chocolate

1. Peel the banana then slice it in half lengthways. Put one of the halves in a small bowl and mash it roughly with a fork and set the other half aside.

2. Put the mashed banana, oats, water and milk in a small saucepan and mix together well. Heat the pan over a low-medium heat for 4–5 minutes, stirring continuously with a wooden spoon, until the porridge has thickened.

3. While the porridge is cooking, slice the remaining banana in half again lengthways. Heat the oil in a small non-stick frying pan over a high heat, then put the banana in the pan flat side down.

4. Pan-fry the banana for 1–2 minutes, or until it is starting to caramelise, then flip it and cook it on the other side for a further minute.

5. Remove both pans from the heat and spoon the porridge into a bowl. Add the caramelised banana slices, then drizzle over the toffee sauce. Grate the dark chocolate over the top, then serve.

CARBONARA
SCRAMBLED EGGS

Who doesn't love a carbonara? Inspired by the flavours of the Roman pasta dish, I've combined Pecorino Romano cheese, pancetta and black pepper with scrambled eggs. A traditional Italian carbonara uses guanciale, which is a cut prepared from pork jowl, but if you can't find it then thick-cut pancetta is a good alternative. The scrambled eggs are spectacular served on toasted sourdough, drizzled with extra virgin olive oil, or even on slices of toasted ciabatta, to continue the Italian theme!

Serves 1 | Preparation time: 15 minutes

½ tsp olive oil

20g thick-cut pancetta, diced (or guanciale, if you can find it)

2 large free-range eggs

20g Pecorino Romano cheese, finely grated, plus 10g extra to serve

pinch each of salt and freshly ground black pepper

1. Heat the oil in a medium non-stick frying pan over a medium heat. Once the oil is hot, add the pancetta and cook for 3–4 minutes, or until it crisps up.

2. Once the pancetta is cooked, drain off some of the fat, then set aside half the pancetta to top the eggs, leaving the rest in the pan. Crack the eggs directly into the pan, then add the grated Pecorino and the salt and pepper.

3. Turn the heat down to low, then use a spatula or wooden spoon to gently push the eggs from the edges of the pan into the centre with a clockwise motion. The uncooked egg will run into the gaps you create, so repeat this motion until the eggs are nearly cooked.

4. Just before the eggs are cooked to your preferred texture, remove the pan from the heat. The eggs will carry on cooking in the residual heat of the pan while you serve, so by the time you tuck into them they will be spot-on. Serve the eggs topped with the remaining pancetta, an extra grating of Pecorino and another pinch of black pepper.

Top Tip

When cooking scrambled eggs, I don't bother to whisk the eggs beforehand, as they are mixed up in the pan anyway and this means less clearing up afterwards! If you prefer, you can whisk the eggs before heating the pan.

PECAN
BAKED OATS

A breakfast that's certain to warm you up on a crisp autumn morning, this will fill your kitchen with a heavenly aroma as it bakes. Blitzing the oats and half the pecan nuts in a blender makes the baked oats more cake-like in texture, but you can leave the oats whole and finely chop the pecans if you prefer.

Serves 1 | Preparation time: 20–25 minutes

coconut oil or butter, for greasing

40g rolled oats

¼ tsp baking powder

30g pecans

½ large ripe banana

½ tsp ground cinnamon

½ tsp ground nutmeg

½ tsp vanilla extract

½ tbsp maple syrup

150ml semi-skimmed milk (or a non-dairy alternative)

1. Preheat your oven to 200°C/180°C fan/gas mark 6. Grease a small baking dish or ramekin with the coconut oil or butter.

2. Put the rolled oats, baking powder and half the pecans into a blender, then blitz them until they are flour-like in texture.

3. In a medium bowl, roughly mash the banana with a fork. Add the blended oat and pecan mixture, cinnamon, nutmeg, vanilla extract, maple syrup and milk, then mix well.

4. Pour the mixture into the baking dish. Roughly chop the remaining pecans and scatter them over the top of the oats.

5. Bake for 15 minutes for a soft texture or 20 minutes for a firmer, cake-like texture. Serve immediately.

CHEDDAR *and* MARMITE
STUFFED FRUFFIN

This may have a silly sounding name, but you'll definitely want to try a fruffin! I coined the word to describe a French toast English muffin. Stuffing the fruffin with Cheddar before pan-frying it gives it a dreamy, melty cheese centre that is revealed as you slice into it. I have added Marmite to the whisked egg, as Cheddar and Marmite are a delightful combination in my opinion, but you can leave this out if you're not a Marmite lover like me!

Serves 1 | Preparation time: 10–15 minutes

1 English muffin

30g mature or extra-mature Cheddar, grated

1 large free-range egg

½ tsp Marmite

pinch each of salt and freshly ground black pepper

1 tsp oil for frying, such as olive oil or cold-pressed rapeseed oil

½ tbsp chives, finely chopped (optional)

1. Use a sharp knife to cut a small circle in the centre of the muffin, leaving about 2cm as a border around the edges. Scoop out the centre of the muffin, then set it aside. Press your fingers lightly against the base and walls of the muffin to create a defined well. Make sure you keep the base and walls of the muffin intact, so the cheese does not leak out during cooking.

2. Put the grated cheese in the well, then put the cut-out centre back on top, pressing down gently with your fingers so that it is level with the top of the muffin.

3. Crack the egg in a medium-sized shallow dish, then add the Marmite and salt and pepper. Beat the mixture with a fork or hand whisk until everything is combined. Soak the muffin on both sides in the mixture, making sure they are well coated.

4. Heat the oil in a medium non-stick frying pan over a medium heat. Once the oil is hot, add the fruffin and cook on each side for 3–4 minutes, or until it is golden and crispy. If the outside of the fruffin looks as though it might burn, turn the heat down to low, to allow enough time for the cheese in the centre to melt.

5. Transfer the fruffin to a plate using a fish slice or spatula, garnish with the chopped chives, if using, then serve.

Top Tip For a churro inspired fruffin, fill the centre with a heaped teaspoon of chocolate spread and roll the fruffin in half a teaspoon each of ground cinnamon and granulated sugar after pan-frying.

Top Tip

Swap the yoghurt for 30g of mascarpone for an indulgent twist.

RASPBERRY *and* WHITE CHOCOLATE **WAFFLE**

The addition of tart raspberries and super-sweet white chocolate chips really elevates the classic waffle in this recipe. If you don't have a waffle maker, the batter works splendidly as pancakes too!

Serves 1 | **Preparation time: 15–20 minutes**

butter or oil, for greasing

40g self-raising flour

1 large free-range egg

40ml semi-skimmed milk (or a non-dairy alternative)

½ tsp vanilla extract

½ tbsp runny honey

20g white chocolate chips

60g raspberries, halved

½ tbsp natural yoghurt

1. Grease your waffle maker with the oil or butter, then preheat it according to the manufacturer's instructions.

2. Put the flour, egg, milk, vanilla extract, honey and most of the chocolate chips in a large mixing bowl, keeping a few chocolate chips for the topping. Mix well until everything is combined.

3. Stir most of the raspberries into the batter, leaving a handful for the topping.

4. Once the waffle maker has reached the right temperature, spoon in the batter in an even layer, then close the lid. Cook for 4–5 minutes, or until the waffle is golden brown and completely cooked though.

5. Carefully remove the waffle using a fish slice or spatula, and transfer it to a plate. Top with the yoghurt, the remaining raspberries and the white chocolate chips. Serve immediately.

HONEY BALSAMIC-
GLAZED HALLOUMI
CRUMPET

Brushing halloumi with a sweet glaze before pan-frying gives it a sticky coating that works superbly with the salty, squeaky cheese. I have combined balsamic vinegar with honey for the glaze, which creates the perfect balance of sharpness and sweetness, and complements the cherry tomatoes too. The avocado and pine nuts are both sources of 'good' fats, which will help to keep you feeling full for longer.

Serves 1 | Preparation time: 10–15 minutes

30g halloumi cheese

½ tsp balsamic vinegar

½ tsp runny honey

½ tsp oil for frying, such as olive oil or cold-pressed rapeseed oil

6 or 7 cherry tomatoes, halved

¼ tsp dried thyme

1 crumpet

½ large avocado, stoned and peeled

pinch each of salt and freshly ground black pepper

15g pine nuts

pinch of chilli flakes, to garnish (optional)

1. Slice the halloumi cheese into ½cm slices using a crinkle knife if possible (see page 28). Mix the vinegar and honey in a small bowl, then brush the glaze all over the halloumi slices, making sure they are evenly coated.

2. Heat the oil in a medium non-stick frying pan over a medium heat. Once the oil is hot, add the slices of halloumi.

3. Fry the halloumi slices on both sides for 1–2 minutes. They may release some water as they cook, but this will evaporate. Make sure you keep a close eye on the halloumi while it is cooking and turn the heat down to low if it looks as though it is starting to burn.

4. Once the halloumi is cooked, remove it from the pan and set it aside. Add the cherry tomatoes and thyme to the pan, then cook them for 2–3 minutes, or until the tomatoes are soft. Turn the heat down to low and put the halloumi back into the pan for a minute to ensure that it's completely warmed through.

5. While the tomatoes are cooking, toast a crumpet and put it on a plate. Mash the avocado in a small bowl with the salt and pepper, then spoon it on top of the crumpet.

6. Top the crumpet with the cooked tomatoes, followed by the halloumi slices, then scatter over the pine nuts. Sprinkle a pinch of chilli flakes on top, if desired, then serve.

Top Tip

This combination is also fabulous served on toast.

PEACHES and CREAM
FROISSANT

Froissant is the name I've given to a French toast croissant (are you starting to see a theme?) and this is well worth a go if you haven't tried one before. The buttery croissant lends itself beautifully to being toasted, remaining soft on the inside with a wonderfully crispy exterior. You can make savoury froissants too, but I've gone for sweet ingredients in this recipe, using honey-glazed peaches, smooth and creamy mascarpone, plus a pinch of thyme to tempt the taste buds.

Serves 1 | **Preparation time: 10–15 minutes**

1 large free-range egg

½ tsp vanilla extract

1 croissant

1 tsp oil for frying, such as coconut oil or cold-pressed rapeseed oil

½ tsp icing sugar

1 medium peach

1 tsp runny honey, plus extra to drizzle

¼ tsp dried thyme (or a few sprigs of fresh thyme), plus extra to garnish

30g mascarpone

1. Crack the egg into a medium-sized shallow dish, then add the vanilla extract. Beat the mixture with a fork until combined.

2. Slice the croissant in half horizontally, then soak both halves in the egg mixture, making sure that both are evenly coated.

3. Heat half the oil in a medium non-stick frying pan over a medium heat. Once the oil is hot, add the froissant halves and cook them for 1–2 minutes on each side, or until they are golden brown and crispy. Transfer the froissant to a plate and dust it with the icing sugar.

4. While the froissant halves are cooking, halve the peach and remove the stone, then slice each half into 1cm-thick slices. Put the remaining oil in another medium non-stick frying pan over a medium heat. Once the oil is hot, add the peach slices, honey and thyme. Cook, stirring occasionally, for 4–5 minutes, or until the slices have softened and are beginning to caramelise.

5. Top the froissant with the mascarpone, then add the peach slices. Drizzle over a little more honey and add an extra pinch of thyme, if desired. Serve immediately.

DIPPY EGGS *and* SMOKY SWEET POTATO **SOLDIERS**

Fancy something a bit different to dip into your soft-boiled eggs? Try these smoky sweet potato soldiers, which can be served as an alternative to toast. Unlike regular potatoes, sweet potatoes do not bind together easily, hence the addition of flour, which has more starch and helps them stick. If you prefer, you can use ordinary potato and leave out the flour for an equally delightful breakfast.

Serves 1 | Preparation time: 15–20 minutes

1 medium sweet potato (about 100g)

½ tbsp plain flour

½ tsp smoked paprika

¼ tsp ground cumin

½ tsp dried rosemary

pinch each of salt and freshly ground black pepper

1 tsp oil for frying, such as olive oil or cold-pressed rapeseed oil

2 large free-range eggs

1. Give the sweet potato a good scrub in cold water. I leave the skin on, but you can peel the potato if you prefer.

2. Grate the potato with a cheese grater, then place it in a clean cloth or tea towel. Squeeze the grated sweet potato as hard as you can over the sink or a large bowl to catch the liquid, until no further liquid comes out.

3. Put the grated potato into a large mixing bowl, then stir in the flour, paprika, cumin, rosemary, salt and pepper, until everything is well combined.

4. Heat the oil in a large non-stick frying pan over a medium heat. Once the oil is hot, spoon the sweet potato into 5 or 6 thin strips, each about 1–1.5cm in width, similar in size to toast soldiers.

5. Cook the soldiers for 4–5 minutes, then carefully flip them using a fish slice or spatula and cook them on the other side for a further 4–5 minutes. At this point they should be crispy on the outside, but if they still look pale cook them for a further minute on both sides.

6. While the soldiers are cooking, fill a medium saucepan with enough water to cover the eggs, then bring it to the boil over a high heat (or speed this up by using freshly boiled water from the kettle).

7. Once the water has reached a rolling boil (large, vigorous bubbles) slowly lower the eggs into the saucepan using a slotted spoon. Keep the water at a rolling boil and set a timer for 5 minutes for room temperature eggs, or 6 minutes for eggs straight from the fridge.

8. Carefully lift the eggs out of the pan with the slotted spoon and immediately place them in egg cups. Remove the tops of the eggs. (My preferred method is my Grandad's trick: tap the top of the egg with a teaspoon to crack the shell, use the handle as a lever to peel the shell from the top half of the egg, then turn the teaspoon round again to slice off the top of the egg.)

9. Serve the eggs with the sweet potato soldiers and start dipping!

Top Tip

Swap the apple for sliced caramelised banana for a banoffee version.

TOFFEE APPLE
LOADED TOAST

Plain toast can be pretty uninspiring, so try slicing it into soldiers and adding your favourite toppings. This is similar to loaded fries, but a breakfast version! It's an easy twist that feels like a treat and will definitely make you want to jump out of bed in the morning. I spread toast with homemade maple butter and add cinnamon-sautéed apples, toffee sauce and chopped pecans, but any sweet or savoury toppings would work – go nuts!

Serves 1 | Preparation time: 10 minutes

1 medium eating apple, cored

½ tsp oil for frying, such as coconut oil or cold-pressed rapeseed oil

¼ tsp ground cinnamon

2 medium slices of white or wholemeal bread

10g salted butter, softened

1 tsp maple syrup

20g pecans, roughly chopped

15g toffee sauce

1. Chop the apple into small pieces about 1cm in size.

2. Heat the oil in a medium non-stick frying pan over a medium heat. Once the oil is hot, add the apple. Sprinkle over the ground cinnamon, then fry for 4–5 minutes, or until the apple has softened and is starting to caramelise.

3. While the apple is cooking, mix the butter and maple syrup in a small bowl. Toast the bread then spread both slices with the maple butter.

4. Slice the toast into soldiers then arrange them on a plate or in a dish. Scatter the cooked cinnamon apple and chopped pecans on top of the toast, then drizzle over the toffee sauce. Serve.

STUFFED
CROISSANT BOATS

Croissants are wonderful as they are, but here's a simple trick to elevate them. Cut out the centres, stuff the gaps with fillings of your choice, then replace the lids before baking them until they are crispy. This is a breakfast that's great to make with children: you can slice the croissants, then they can help by choosing their favourite fillings and stuffing the croissants before you place them in the oven to bake.

Serves 2 | Preparation time: 10–15 minutes

2 croissants

60g mature or extra-mature Cheddar, grated

2 spring onions, chopped into 1cm pieces

10g melted butter

1. Preheat your oven to 190°C/170°C/gas mark 5. Line a baking tray with baking paper.

2. Use a sharp knife to cut out the centre of one of the croissants, leaving a border around the edges. Scoop out the centre of the croissant, then set it aside. Press your fingers lightly against the base and sides of the croissant to create a defined well, making sure you keep them intact so the fillings do not leak out while cooking. Repeat with the remaining croissant.

3. Place both croissants on the baking tray, then put the Cheddar and spring onion in the wells, dividing them evenly between the two. Press the cut-out centre back on top of each croissant, then brush them all over with the melted butter.

4. Bake for 10 minutes, or until the croissants are golden brown and crispy and the cheese is melted.

5. Transfer the croissants to plates using a fish slice or spatula, then serve immediately.

Top Tip

Try swapping the spring onion for a few quartered cherry tomatoes or a handful of washed baby spinach. For a sweet and gooey version, try adding a spoonful of Nutella and a handful of mini marshmallows.

PIÑA COLADA
PORRIDGE

A piña colada is one of my favourite cocktails, so I have included the flavours of that delicious drink in this porridge recipe – but not the rum! Using tinned pineapple (in juice, rather than syrup) is an easy shortcut, and the juice from the tin will enhance the pineapple flavour of the porridge. The tropical taste will temporarily transport you to the beach, even if you're eating this on a gloomy morning before a busy day!

Serves 1 | Preparation time: 10 minutes

2 tinned pineapple rings, plus 50ml juice from the tin

40g rolled oats

75ml cold water

125ml coconut milk drink

1 tsp runny honey

½ tsp coconut oil (or another oil), for frying

½ tbsp coconut yoghurt

15g coconut flakes or desiccated coconut

1. Slice one pineapple ring into 1cm pieces and leave the other whole.

2. Put the oats, water, coconut milk drink, honey and pineapple juice in a small saucepan and mix well. Heat the pan over a low-medium heat for 4–5 minutes, stirring the mixture continuously with a wooden spoon, until the porridge has thickened.

3. While the porridge is cooking, heat the oil in a small non-stick frying pan over a high heat. Once the oil is hot put the whole pineapple ring in the pan. Cook it for 1–2 minutes, or until the pineapple is starting to caramelise, then flip it and cook it on the other side for a further minute.

4. Remove the saucepan from the heat and spoon the porridge into a bowl. Top the porridge with the caramelised pineapple ring, chopped pineapple, coconut yoghurt, coconut flakes or desiccated coconut, then serve.

LAZY DAYS
and
SUNDAYS

SAVOURY BREAKFAST TACO
SHARING BOARD

This is an easy, fun idea for a family breakfast – or if you have guests for breakfast or brunch. Everyone can build their own mini breakfast tacos with their favourite fillings, making this a real crowd-pleaser. You can use my suggested fillings listed below or come up with your own. I recommend preparing cold ingredients, such as the grated cheese or chopped tomatoes, in advance, and cooking the warm components, such as the tacos and scrambled eggs, immediately before serving. Don't forget to check out my French toast tacos on the next page for a scrummy sweet version!

Serves 4 | **Preparation time: 30–35 minutes**

For the tacos

4 large wheat tortilla wraps

For the fillings

scrambled eggs (see page 14)

avocado, mashed or sliced, with a pinch of chilli flakes (optional) and lemon or lime wedges to squeeze

cherry tomatoes, quartered

red or yellow peppers, cored and diced

spring onions, finely chopped

pan-fried chorizo, diced or sliced into rounds, or bacon lardons

grated cheese, such as mozzarella or mature Cheddar

sweet chilli sauce or hot sauce

sour cream or crème fraîche

fresh coriander, roughly chopped

1. Preheat your oven to 200°C/180°C fan/gas mark 6.

2. Place a tortilla wrap on a chopping board, then cut small circles in the wrap with a sharp knife, using a ramekin, the rim of a mug or an egg ring as a template. You should be able to get at least 4 small circles from each wrap. Repeat with the remaining 3 wraps.

3. Turn a 12-hole muffin tin upside down on your kitchen worktop. The spaces between the raised cups on the underside of the tin are ideal for shaping the tortilla circles into mini tacos which will retain their shape when baked. Gently press each tortilla circle into a gap, placing as many as you can on the tin without overlapping them. You may need to do this in batches if you are making more than 16.

4. Place the upside-down tin in the oven and bake the tacos for 8 minutes, or until they are golden and crispy. Repeat with the remaining tortilla circles.

5. Allow the mini tacos to cool slightly before carefully removing them from the muffin tin. Arrange the tacos on a large serving board or plate with your choice of fillings, then serve.

Top Tip

Don't throw away the leftover pieces of the tortilla wraps; use them to make homemade tortilla crisps! Cut them into triangles, season with salt (or half a teaspoon of fajita seasoning), pour a drizzle of oil over the top, then arrange them in a single layer on a baking tray and bake at 200°C/180°C fan/gas mark 6 for 8 minutes.

SWEET BREAKFAST TACO
SHARING BOARD

This is another fun-filled breakfast or brunch that's sure to impress! It's a sweet version of my savoury breakfast taco sharing board on the previous page, with an additional French toast twist. You could even serve it as a breakfast 'dessert' following the savoury tacos, if they go down a storm. Simply place the board in the middle of the table and let everyone dig in!

Serves 4 | **Preparation time: 30–35 minutes**

For the tacos

4 large wheat tortilla wraps

butter or oil, for greasing

1 large free-range egg

½ tsp vanilla extract

1 tsp icing sugar, plus extra for dusting

For the fillings

chopped fruit, such as strawberries, raspberries, banana, whole blueberries, clementine segments

natural or Greek yoghurt

maple syrup or runny honey

sweet spreads, such as Nutella, peanut butter, jam or Lotus Biscoff spread

chopped nuts, such as pecans, cashews, almonds, hazelnuts

chocolate chips (milk, white or dark)

dried fruit, such as raisins, sultanas, blueberries, cherries or mango

desiccated coconut

mini marshmallows

hundreds and thousands or sugar sprinkles

1. Preheat your oven to 200°C/180°C fan/gas mark 6.

2. Place a tortilla wrap on a chopping board, then cut small circles in the wrap with a sharp knife, using a ramekin, the rim of a mug or an egg ring as a template. You should be able to get at least 4 small circles out of each wrap. Repeat with the remaining 3 wraps.

3. Turn a 12-hole muffin tin upside down on your kitchen worktop. The spaces between the raised cups on the underside of the tin are ideal for shaping the tortilla circles into mini tacos which will retain their shape when baked. Grease between the raised cups and the bottom of the tin with the butter or oil.

4. Crack the egg into a medium shallow bowl then beat it with a fork or hand whisk. Add the vanilla extract and sugar, then mix well. Dip each tortilla circle into the whisked egg and allow any excess to run off. Gently press the tortilla circles into the gaps between the cups of the upside-down tin to create a taco shape. Place as many as you can on the tin without overlapping them. You may need to do this in batches if you are making more than 16.

5. Place the upside-down tin in the oven and bake the tacos for 8 minutes, or until they are golden and crispy. Repeat with any remaining tortilla circles.

6. Allow the mini tacos to cool slightly before carefully removing them from the muffin tin. Dust them all over with the icing sugar then arrange them on a large serving board or plate. Add your preferred fillings, then serve.

Top Tip

Stir a teaspoon of Marmite into the grated potato for an umami boost or, alternatively, add a teaspoon of green or red pesto to the potato and swap the Cheddar for grated mozzarella.

MELT-IN-THE-MIDDLE
HASH BROWNS

How do you make my homemade hash browns (see page 27) even more irresistible? Give them a hidden cheese middle that oozes as you slice into them! Crispy and golden on the outside, with an indulgent cheese centre, these hash browns may be simple in terms of ingredients, but they are powerful when it comes to flavour! I use Cheddar for the melting middles, but any hard cheese will work. Try swapping it for some grated Gruyère, red Leicester or mozzarella – or even a combination of different cheeses.

Serves 1 (makes 3 hash browns; can be served as a side dish) |
Preparation time: 20–25 minutes

1 large potato (220–240g), preferably a floury, non-waxy variety, such as Maris Piper or King Edward

pinch each of salt and freshly ground black pepper

1 tsp dried rosemary

½ tbsp oil for frying, such as olive oil or cold-pressed rapeseed oil

30g mature or extra-mature Cheddar cheese, grated

½ tbsp chives, finely chopped (optional)

1. Give the potato a good scrub in cold water. I leave the skin on, but you can peel it if you prefer.

2. Grate the potato, then place it in a clean cloth or tea towel. Squeeze the potato as hard as you can over the sink or a large bowl to catch the excess liquid, until no further liquid comes out. Make sure not to skip this step, or the hash browns will be soggy and less likely to bind together as a result.

3. Put the grated potato into a large mixing bowl and stir in the salt, pepper and rosemary.

4. Heat the oil in a large non-stick frying pan over a medium-high heat. Once the oil is hot, spoon half the potato into 3 circular shapes. You can use greased egg or crumpet rings for neat hash browns, or shape them freestyle.

5. Distribute the grated cheese evenly between the hash browns, placing some in the centre of each, then spoon the remaining grated potato on top, making sure that the cheese centres are completely covered.

6. Cook the hash browns for 3–4 minutes, then carefully flip them using a fish slice or spatula, and cook them for a further 3–4 minutes. At this point, the hash browns should be golden and crispy on the outside, but if they are looking pale, cook them for a further minute on both sides.

7. Transfer the hash browns to a plate with a fish slice or spatula, then sprinkle over the chopped chives, if desired. Serve immediately.

CARROT CAKE
PANCAKES

Cake for breakfast? Yes please! OK, it might not be an actual cake, but this fluffy stack of pancakes replicates the warming flavours of a carrot cake, with an indulgent cream cheese frosting that definitely feels a treat at breakfast time. And the addition of the grated carrot means you are getting one of your five-a-day first thing – winner!

Serves 1 | Preparation time: 20–25 minutes

1 medium carrot (90–100g)

40g self-raising flour

½ tsp ground cinnamon

¼ tsp ground nutmeg

¼ tsp ground ginger

zest and juice of ½ large orange, plus extra zest to garnish

½ tbsp maple syrup

40ml semi-skimmed milk (or a non-dairy alternative)

1 large free-range egg

½ tsp oil for frying, such as coconut oil or cold-pressed rapeseed oil

For the frosting

10ml double cream

20g cream cheese

½ tsp icing sugar or maple syrup

20g walnuts, roughly chopped

1. Give the carrot a good scrub, then cut off the top. Grate it with a cheese grater, then put it in a large mixing bowl.

2. Add the flour, cinnamon, nutmeg, ginger, orange zest and juice, maple syrup and milk to the bowl, then mix well.

3. Separate the egg, mixing the yolk into the batter. Put the egg white in a separate mixing bowl, then beat it with an electric whisk until it forms stiff peaks. Gently fold the egg white into the pancake batter, making sure not to knock out too much of the air you've whisked in.

4. Heat the oil in a large non-stick frying pan over a medium heat. Once the oil is hot, spoon the batter into the pan, using about one tablespoon per pancake. Make sure you leave a small gap between each pancake as they will spread slightly as they cook.

5. Cook the pancakes for 1–2 minutes, or until tiny bubbles start to appear on the surface, then carefully flip them using a fish slice or spatula and cook for a further 1–2 minutes. Repeat until you have used all the batter (you may need to do this in batches, depending on the size of your pan).

6. While the pancakes are cooking, prepare the frosting by whisking the double cream, cream cheese and icing sugar together in a bowl, using a hand or electric whisk.

7. Stack the pancakes on a plate, spreading some frosting between each one, then top them with the remaining frosting, chopped walnuts and some additional orange zest, if desired. Serve.

SUN-DRIED TOMATO *and* THREE CHEESE
BAGEL STRATA

This recipe is impressive served as a weekend breakfast or brunch – it's a bit like a savoury breakfast cake. Bagels work really well in this dish because they keep some of their chewy texture, giving it much needed structure. This is big in flavour and you'll definitely want to go back for more slices, if it hasn't all been scoffed!

Serves 4–6 | Preparation time: 50–55 minutes

butter or oil, for greasing

4 bagels

3 large free-range eggs

150ml semi-skimmed milk (or a non-dairy alternative)

½ tsp dried oregano

½ tbsp fresh basil leaves, roughly torn, plus extra to garnish

pinch each of salt and freshly ground black pepper

30g Pecorino Romano cheese, grated

60g Parmigiano Reggiano cheese, grated

90g mozzarella cheese, grated

145g sun-dried tomatoes in oil, drained and roughly chopped

1. Preheat your oven to 200°C/180°C fan/gas mark 6, then grease a 20cm non-stick springform cake tin with the butter or oil. Line the base of the tin with baking paper.

2. Tear or slice the bagels into pieces about 2–2.5cm in size.

3. In a large mixing bowl, beat the eggs with the milk, oregano, basil and salt and pepper with a hand whisk or fork until combined. Add the grated cheese (keeping a handful to top the strata), sun-dried tomatoes and bagel pieces to the bowl. Give the mixture a good stir to make sure all the ingredients are combined, then leave it to sit for a few minutes so the bagels absorb the egg mixture.

4. Pour the mixture into the cake tin, then top it with the remaining grated cheese. Bake the strata for 35–40 minutes, or until it is golden brown. You can check if it is cooked by inserting a skewer into the centre, which should come out clean. If not, bake the strata for a further 5 minutes.

5. Remove the tin from the oven, then leave it to cool slightly before opening the tin to release the sides. Carefully lift the strata from the base and place it on a plate. Garnish it with extra torn basil then serve immediately. Alternatively, allow the strata to cool completely on a wire rack before transferring it to an airtight container to store in the fridge for up to 3 days. It can be frozen for up to 3 months; slice it before freezing and put greaseproof paper between the slices to prevent them sticking to each other.

Top Tip **Use the oil from the sun-dried tomatoes to grease the cake tin for extra flavour!**

BIRTHDAY CAKE
FRUMPET STACK

My birthday-cake themed frumpets (French toast crumpets) are a terrific way to start your special day, especially if you can persuade a loved one to prepare them and serve them to you as breakfast in bed. You could even add a candle on top!

Serves 1 | Preparation time: 10–15 minutes

1 large free-range egg

1 tsp vanilla extract

1 tsp icing sugar

2 crumpets

1 tsp oil for frying, such as coconut oil or cold-pressed rapeseed oil

For the toppings

30ml whipping cream

20g strawberry jam

½ tsp icing sugar

80g fresh fruit or berries, such as strawberries, raspberries or blueberries

1 tsp hundreds and thousands or sugar sprinkles, to decorate (optional)

1. Crack the egg into a medium shallow bowl, then beat it with a fork or hand whisk. Add the vanilla extract and icing sugar, then mix well.

2. Soak the crumpets in the egg mixture on both sides for 1 minute, making sure that they are completely coated.

3. Heat the oil in a large non-stick frying pan over a medium heat. Once the oil is hot, add the frumpets and fry them for 2–3 minutes on each side, or until they are golden brown and crispy.

4. While the frumpets are cooking, beat the whipping cream with an electric whisk until it forms stiff peaks, then set it aside.

5. Place one of the frumpets on a plate, spread it with strawberry jam then half the whipped cream. Put the other frumpet on top, then dust them with icing sugar. Top with the remaining whipped cream, fresh fruit and hundreds and thousands or sugar sprinkles, if desired, then serve.

Top Tip

Add 1 tsp cocoa powder to the whisked egg for chocolate-flavoured frumpets.

Top Tip **For a veggie version, swap the bacon for a poached egg, or leave it out altogether.**

COURGETTE, FETA *and* LEMON
FRITTERS

These fabulous fritters make a wonderful brunch – the tangy feta and lemon zest really lifts the flavour. They are especially tasty topped with crispy bacon lardons!

Serves 1 | Preparation time: 20–25 minutes

1 medium or ½ large courgette

½ tbsp plain flour

pinch each of salt and freshly ground black pepper

zest of ½ large lemon, plus extra to garnish

½ tsp dried oregano

1 large free-range egg

30g feta cheese

1 tsp oil for frying, such as olive oil or cold-pressed rapeseed oil

30g unsmoked or smoked bacon lardons

1 tsp chives, finely chopped (optional)

1. Grate the courgette with a cheese grater, then place it in a clean cloth or tea towel. Squeeze the grated courgette as hard as you can over the sink or a large bowl to catch the excess liquid, until no further liquid comes out.

2. Put the grated courgette in a large mixing bowl. Add the flour, salt and pepper, lemon zest, oregano and egg, then give it all a good stir. Crumble most of the feta into the bowl, keeping a handful to top the fritters, then mix until everything is combined.

3. Heat the oil in a large non-stick frying pan over a medium-high heat. Once the oil is hot, spoon the batter into the pan – using about one tablespoon per fritter. The batter should make 6–7 fritters; you may need to cook them in batches depending on the size of your pan.

4. Cook the fritters for 2–3 minutes, or until they are golden on both sides, carefully flipping them with a fish slice or spatula. Remove the fritters from the pan, then place them on a plate in a very low oven to keep warm while you cook the bacon.

5. Put the bacon lardons in the same pan, then fry them over a medium heat for 3–4 minutes, or until they are crispy. Stack the fritters and top them with the bacon, the remaining feta, an extra grating of lemon zest and the chopped chives, if using. Serve immediately.

MINI EGG
HOT CROSS BUN BAKE

I absolutely adore hot cross buns, so this bake is my ideal breakfast on Easter Sunday morning. You can use any type of hot cross bun – there are some incredible flavours available in the major supermarkets. I use half classic hot cross buns and half double-chocolate ones, for a scrumptious combination!

Serves 6 | Preparation time: 40–45 minutes

butter, for greasing

6 hot cross buns, any flavour

2 large free-range eggs

150ml semi-skimmed milk (or a non-dairy alternative)

zest and juice of 1 large orange

½ tsp ground cinnamon

¼ tsp ground nutmeg

½ tbsp granulated sugar

80g mini eggs (or another chocolate of your choice), roughly chopped

For the cross on top (optional)

1 tsp plain flour

½ tsp cold water

1. Preheat your oven to 180°C/ 160°C fan/gas mark 4, then grease a large baking dish or a tin with butter.

2. Tear or slice the hot cross buns into pieces about 2cm in size.

3. In a large mixing bowl, beat the eggs with the milk, orange zest and juice, spices and sugar, using a hand whisk or fork. Add the hot cross bun pieces, give the mixture a good stir to make sure everything is combined, then leave it to sit for a few minutes so the hot cross bun pieces absorb the egg mixture.

4. Tip the mixture into the baking dish, then scatter over the mini eggs. To add a cross, mix the flour and cold water in a small bowl, then transfer the mixture to a piping bag (or use a sandwich bag with a hole cut in the corner). Pipe a cross shape on top of the bake.

5. Bake for 30–35 minutes, or until the bake is golden brown, then serve it immediately.

Top Tip

Swap the mini eggs for chocolate orange mini eggs (or chunks of chocolate orange Easter egg), for a more intense flavour.

FRENCH TOAST
NACHOS

Here's my breakfast take on nachos, using French toast cut into triangles instead of tortilla crisps, and adding ingredients that you might find in a cooked breakfast – such as bacon, tomatoes and baked beans – as toppings. You can also include other breakfast items, such as sliced cooked sausages, hash browns, black pudding or scrambled eggs. Load it up! Although this recipe serves one, you could prepare it for a big family brunch too – simply scale up the ingredients, use a large ovenproof dish, then place it on the table for everyone to get stuck in!

Serves 1 | Preparation time: 20–25 minutes

1 large free-range egg

20ml semi-skimmed milk (or a non-dairy alternative)

pinch each of salt and freshly ground black pepper

2 medium slices of white or wholemeal bread

1 tsp oil for frying, such as olive oil or cold-pressed rapeseed oil

30g smoked or unsmoked bacon lardons, or 2 rashers streaky bacon, diced

80g baked beans

¼ tsp smoked paprika

5 or 6 cherry tomatoes, quartered

30g grated cheese, such as mature Cheddar or mozzarella

½ tbsp chives, finely chopped (optional)

1. Crack the egg into a medium shallow bowl, then beat it with the milk and salt and pepper, using a fork or hand whisk. Soak both slices of bread on both sides in the egg mixture, and allow any excess to run off.

2. Heat the oil in a large non-stick frying pan over a medium-high heat. Once the oil is hot, add both slices of bread. Cook them for 1–2 minutes on each side, or until they are golden and crispy.

3. Remove the French toast from the pan using a fish slice or spatula, and allow it to cool slightly before slicing into small triangles. Arrange the triangles in a small ovenproof baking dish.

4. Heat the same frying pan over a medium heat and add the bacon. Fry the bacon for 3–4 minutes, or until it is crispy and completely cooked through.

5. While the bacon is cooking, heat the baked beans with the paprika in a small saucepan over a medium heat, stirring regularly with a wooden spoon, until they are piping hot.

6. Spoon the beans over the French toast triangles, then scatter over the tomatoes, bacon and grated cheese. Heat the grill to medium hot.

7. Place the dish under the grill until the cheese is bubbling and completely melted. Garnish with the chopped chives, if using, then serve.

Top Tip

Swap the bread for crumpets for a frumpet version!

CHEESY CHIVE **POTATO WAFFLE**
with SOUR CREAM *and* SMOKED BACON

This cheesy chive potato waffle can be served for brunch as it is, but is equally scrumptious with the addition of fried or poached eggs. Microwaving the potato rather than peeling and boiling it saves time, but you could also use leftover mashed potato if you have it.

Serves 1 | Preparation time: 20–25 minutes

butter or oil, for greasing

1 large potato (220–240g), preferably a floury, non-waxy variety such as Maris Piper or King Edward

1 large free-range egg

30g mature or extra-mature Cheddar cheese, grated

½ tbsp chives, finely chopped, plus extra to garnish

½ tsp dried rosemary

pinch each of salt and freshly ground black pepper

30g smoked bacon lardons, or 2 rashers smoked streaky bacon, diced

½ tbsp sour cream

1. Grease your waffle maker with the oil or butter, then preheat it according to the manufacturer's instructions.

2. Give the potato a good scrub, then prick the skin all over with a fork. Place it on a microwaveable plate and microwave on high for 6–7 minutes, or until the potato is cooked through. Set it aside until it is cool enough to handle without burning your fingers.

3. Slice the potato in half, then scoop out the flesh with a spoon and put it in a large mixing bowl. Mash the potato with a fork, then add the egg, grated Cheddar, chives, rosemary, salt and pepper and mix well.

4. Once the waffle maker has reached the appropriate temperature, spoon in the potato mixture in an even layer, then close the lid. Cook for 5–6 minutes, or until the waffle is golden brown and completely cooked though.

5. While the waffle is cooking, heat a medium non-stick frying pan over a medium heat. Add the bacon and fry it for 3–4 minutes, or until it is crispy.

6. Carefully remove the waffle using a fish slice or spatula, and transfer it to a plate. Top with the sour cream, followed by the crispy bacon and some extra chopped chives, to garnish. Serve immediately.

HOMEMADE
MINI POP TARTS

This homemade version of the sugary American breakfast treat isn't too tricky to prepare if you use ready-rolled shortcrust pastry. It's a fun recipe for involving the kids, especially the decorating part. I like to make mini pop tarts with different flavoured jam fillings, but feel free to add other fillings, such as Nutella or mashed fruit for a healthier version.

Serves 4 (makes 16 mini pop tarts) |
Preparation time: 40 minutes, plus at least 30 minutes cooling time

plain flour, for dusting

1 sheet (375g) ready-rolled shortcrust pastry

16 tsp jam of your choice (I use half strawberry and half blueberry jam)

1 large free-range egg, beaten

For the topping

50g icing sugar

2 tsp cold water

hundreds and thousands or sugar sprinkles, to decorate

1. Preheat your oven to 200°C/180°C fan/gas mark 6.

2. Unroll the sheet of shortcrust pastry on a floured board or surface. Cut the pastry in half vertically, then in half again so you have 4 rectangles. Cut each rectangle in half into 8 rectangles, then cut these horizontally, so you end up with 16 evenly-sized rectangles.

3. Put one teaspoon of jam on the top half of each vertical pastry rectangle, leaving a small border around the edges. Brush the borders of the pastry with the beaten egg, then gently fold over the remaining half of the pastry so the jam is completely covered. Press firmly around the edges to ensure that jam doesn't leak out during cooking.

4. Use a fork to crimp the edges of the pastry, then brush the pop tarts all over with the egg wash. Prick a few holes in the top of each pop tart with a skewer to allow steam to escape during cooking.

5. Bake the tarts for 15–20 minutes, or until the pastry is golden brown, then remove them from the oven and leave them to cool completely on a wire rack for at least 30 minutes.

6. Prepare the glaze by gradually adding the cold water to the icing sugar in a small bowl, a drop at a time, until you have a runny consistency. Spoon a small amount of the glaze on to the centre of each pop tart, then scatter over the hundreds and thousands or sugar sprinkles.

7. Either serve the tarts immediately or transfer them to an airtight container. They will keep at room temperature for up to 3 days.

TOAD IN THE
CROISSANT

My breakfast twist on the British classic toad in the hole is the best kind of way to start a lazy Sunday. I have swapped the Yorkshire pudding batter for whisked eggs mixed with chunks of chopped up croissants, which gives the dish a French toast vibe. I used pork sausages, but feel free to use any type of sausages, meat or veggie. The recipe serves four, but the ingredients can easily be increased or reduced, depending on how many you are cooking for. You can either enjoy the bake as it is, with tomato ketchup, brown sauce or sweet chilli sauce, or serve it with warm baked beans, cooked tomatoes or mushrooms, for a filling brunch.

Serves 4 | Preparation time: 40–45 minutes

4 good-quality pork sausages

½ tsp oil for roasting, such as olive oil or cold-pressed rapeseed oil

4 croissants

3 large free-range eggs

50ml semi-skimmed milk (or a non-dairy alternative)

pinch each of salt and freshly ground black pepper

½ tsp chopped sage (fresh or dried)

¼ tsp chopped thyme (fresh or dried)

1. Preheat your oven to 220°C/200°C fan/gas mark 7.

2. Place the sausages in a medium baking dish or tin, then drizzle over the oil. Roast the sausages for 15 minutes, turning them halfway through the cooking time.

3. While the sausages are cooking, slice the croissants into pieces about 2cm in size.

4. In a large mixing bowl, beat the eggs with the milk, salt and pepper, sage and thyme, using a hand whisk or fork. Add the croissant pieces to the bowl, give the mixture a good stir to make sure everything is combined, then leave it to sit for a few minutes so the croissants absorb the egg mixture.

5. Remove the sausages from the oven and pour the egg-soaked croissant mixture over them, making sure it is evenly distributed around the tin.

6. Bake for a further 20–25 minutes, or until the sausages are completely cooked through and the croissants are puffed up and golden, then serve immediately.

Top Tip

Upgrade the recipe by wrapping a rasher of unsmoked streaky bacon around each sausage for a pigs-in-blankets version. Alternatively, swap the croissants for 4 chopped-up crumpets for toad in the crumpet, which is also worth a try!

Top Tip

If you need to cook the pancakes in batches, put the cooked pancakes on a plate in the oven on a very low heat to keep them warm.

GIN *and* TONIC
PANCAKES

Gin and tonic may not be a typical breakfast drink, but how about adding it to your pancakes? These grown-up pancakes are definitely not suitable for children, but are glorious served at a boozy brunch or celebration. If you prefer a non-alcoholic version, you can swap the gin in the pancakes for a 0% alcohol gin, or leave it out completely and replace the gin with extra tonic water.

Serves 1 | Preparation time: 20 minutes

40g self-raising flour

1 tsp granulated sugar

zest of ½ lime or lemon, plus extra to decorate

40ml tonic water

1 tbsp gin of your choice

1 large free-range egg

½ tsp oil for frying, such as coconut oil or cold-pressed rapeseed oil

For the toppings

½ tbsp icing sugar

juice of ½ lime or lemon

½ tbsp gin of your choice

1 tbsp tonic water

80g raspberries, halved

1. Put the self-raising flour, sugar, lime or lemon zest, tonic water and gin in a large mixing bowl then mix well.

2. Separate the egg, mixing the yolk into the batter. Put the egg white into a separate mixing bowl, then beat it with an electric whisk until it forms stiff peaks. Gently fold the egg white into the pancake batter, making sure not to knock out too much of the air you whisked in.

3. Heat the oil in a large non-stick frying pan over a medium heat. Once the oil is hot, spoon the batter into the pan, using about one tablespoon per pancake. Make sure you leave a small gap between the pancakes as they will spread slightly as they cook.

4. Cook the pancakes for 1–2 minutes, or until tiny bubbles start to appear on the surface, then carefully flip them using a fish slice or spatula, and cook for a further 1–2 minutes on the other side. Repeat until you have used all the batter (you may need to do this in batches, depending on the size of your pan).

5. While the pancakes are cooking, prepare the drizzle by mixing the icing sugar, lime or lemon juice, gin and tonic water in a small bowl.

6. Once all pancakes are cooked, transfer them to a plate and use a skewer or toothpick to pierce a few small holes in each pancake, then pour over the drizzle. Stack the pancakes, top with the raspberries and grate over some extra lime or lemon zest, then serve.

CHEESY GARLIC
CRUMPET BAKE

As you may already know, I'm an enormous fan of crumpets and use them frequently in my breakfast recipes. I initially came up with the idea of a crumpet bake in 2017. This is my savoury take on a classic bread and butter pudding, but breakfast-style, swapping the bread for crumpets and adding bacon, Cheddar and wilted spinach. I posted my recipe on Instagram and it was such a hit that I started creating different versions, both savoury and sweet, which I have continued to share over the past five years. I just had to include a version of one of my signature recipes in this book, so here is my new favourite: a cheesy garlic crumpet bake. If you have enjoyed any of my crumpet bake recipes, you'll love this one too!

Serves 3–6 | **Preparation time: 40 minutes**

45g softened salted butter, plus extra for greasing

6 crumpets

1 clove garlic, crushed or finely chopped

½ tbsp parsley, very finely chopped

90g mozzarella cheese, grated

3 large free-range eggs

50ml semi-skimmed milk (or a non-dairy alternative)

pinch each of salt and freshly ground black pepper

1. Preheat your oven to 200°C/180°C fan/gas mark 6 then grease a large baking dish with butter.

2. Lightly toast the crumpets, then set them aside.

3. Mix together the butter, garlic and parsley in a small bowl, then spread the butter on the crumpets, dividing it evenly between them. Slice each crumpet in half, then arrange them face upwards in the baking dish. Sprinkle over the grated mozzarella, tucking some in between each crumpet half.

4. Crack the eggs into a large jug, then add the milk and salt and pepper. Beat the mixture with a fork or hand whisk until everything is combined, then pour it over the crumpets. Leave them to soak for a couple of minutes.

5. Bake for 30 minutes, or until the top is golden brown and bubbling, then serve immediately.

Top Tip

Make this even tastier by sprinkling over roughly chopped cooked bacon before serving.

GINGER HASSELBACK
BAKED PEARS

This delicious dish uses the Hasselback technique (see page 74 for my Caprese Hasselback Croissant recipe) but this time I've based it on baked pears, which works fantastically well. I serve the pears for breakfast with natural yoghurt and granola, but they are also fab added to porridge, pancakes or waffles, and could even be served as a dessert with vanilla ice cream.

Serves 2 | Preparation time: 25–30 minutes

2 Conference pears, cored

1 tsp melted butter or oil for roasting, such as coconut oil or cold-pressed rapeseed oil

½ tbsp maple syrup

½ tsp ground cinnamon

½ tsp ground ginger

1. Preheat your oven to 200°C/180°C fan/gas mark 6. Line a baking tray with baking paper.

2. On a chopping board, slice a pear in half using a sharp knife. With the flat side facing down, make slices a few millimetres apart along the halves, making sure not to cut all the way through. Repeat with the remaining half and the second pear, then place the 4 halves on the baking tray.

3. In a small bowl, mix the butter or oil with the maple syrup, cinnamon and ginger, then brush the mixture all over the pears.

4. Bake for 20–25 minutes, or until the pears have softened and are beginning to caramelise, basting halfway through cooking with any remaining ginger spice mixture.

5. Remove the baking tray from the oven and serve the pears immediately.

Top Tip
Try swapping the pears for eating apples instead. Follow the same method, but cook the apples for 10 minutes longer.

DIPPY EGGS *with* MAPLE *and* THYME-ROASTED CARROT SOLDIERS

Forget toast and try dipping these roasted carrots into your soft-boiled eggs instead! Roasting carrots in the oven turns the humble root vegetable into something special, making them caramelised and tender, while the maple syrup enhances their natural sweetness as well as giving them a sticky glaze. The oven does most of the work, so you can head back to bed with the papers while you wait for the carrots to roast, making this breakfast ideal for a lazy weekend.

Serves 2 | Preparation time: 45 minutes

2 medium carrots (100g each)

½ tbsp oil for roasting, such as olive oil, coconut oil or cold-pressed rapeseed oil

½ tbsp maple syrup

½ tsp dried thyme

¼ tsp ground nutmeg

pinch each of salt and freshly ground black pepper

4 large free-range eggs

1. Preheat your oven to 200°C/180°C fan/gas mark 6.

2. Scrub the carrots in cold water then remove the tops. Slice the carrots in half, then into batons about 1cm thick.

3. Put the carrot batons into a large roasting tin or baking tray. Toss them with the oil, maple syrup, thyme, nutmeg and salt and pepper, then arrange them in a single layer.

4. Roast for 25 minutes, remove them from the oven and turn them, then return to the oven for a further 10 minutes. The carrots are ready once they are tender enough to be pierced with a fork.

5. While the carrots are in the oven for the final 10 minutes, fill a large saucepan with enough water to cover the eggs, then bring it to the boil over a high heat. To speed this up, you can use freshly boiled water from the kettle.

6. Once the water has reached a rolling boil (large, vigorous bubbles), slowly lower your eggs into the saucepan, using a slotted spoon. Keep the water on a rolling boil and set a timer to cook the eggs for 5 minutes for room temperature eggs, or for 6 minutes for eggs straight from the fridge.

7. Carefully lift the eggs out of the pan using a slotted spoon and immediately place them in egg cups. Remove the tops of the eggs. (My preferred method is my Grandad's trick: tap the top of the egg with a teaspoon to crack the shell, use the handle of the teaspoon as a lever to peel the shell from the top half of the egg, then turn the teaspoon round again and use it to slice off the top of the egg.)

8. Serve the eggs with the carrot soldiers and start dipping!

Top Tip The carrots can also be served as a side dish with your Sunday roast. Why not prepare a large batch and freeze the leftovers to defrost and gently reheat at a later date?

MINCE PIE
PORRIDGE

Like Christmas in a bowl, this cosy porridge showcases the fruity, spiced flavours of a mince pie. I like to serve this porridge on a chilly December morning, as a way to use up mincemeat left over from baking homemade mince pies.

Serves 1 | Preparation time: 10 minutes

1 medium eating apple, cored and grated

40g rolled oats

15g raisins or currants (optional)

½ tsp vanilla extract

¼ tsp ground cinnamon, plus extra to garnish

¼ tsp ground nutmeg

¼ tsp mixed spice

zest of ¼ lemon, plus extra to garnish

125ml semi-skimmed milk (or a non-dairy alternative)

125ml cold water

1 tsp mincemeat

1. Combine the grated apple (keeping a little to top the porridge), oats, raisins or currants, if using, vanilla extract, spices, lemon zest, milk and water in a small saucepan.

2. Heat the pan over a low-medium heat for 4–5 minutes, stirring continuously with a wooden spoon, until the porridge has thickened.

3. Remove the pan from the heat and spoon the porridge into a bowl. Top with the remaining grated apple, mincemeat, an extra dusting of cinnamon and a little more grated lemon zest. Serve.

Top Tip

Try using orange zest instead of lemon zest for an equally delicious twist.

FESTIVE SAUSAGE *and* EGG
MUFFIN

My homemade sausage and egg muffin is an excellent hangover cure when you're nursing a sore head from one too many Christmas parties! It's also a great way of using up leftover cooked stuffing from a Sunday roast or Christmas dinner. The herby flavours of the stuffing work brilliantly with the pork sausage, while the parsnip hash brown and cranberry sauce provide a fantastic balance with their sweetness.

Serves 2 | **Preparation time: 35—40 minutes**

2 good-quality pork sausages

45g cooked stuffing

2½ tsp oil for frying, such as olive oil or cold-pressed rapeseed oil

1 medium potato (120–130g), preferably a floury, non-waxy variety, such as Maris Piper or King Edward

1 medium parsnip

pinch each of salt and freshly ground black pepper

2 large free-range eggs

2 English muffins

2 tsp cranberry sauce

1. Squeeze the meat out of the casing of the sausages, then combine it in a small bowl with the cooked stuffing. Divide the mixture in half and shape into patties that are slightly bigger in diameter than the muffins (they will shrink as they cook).

2. Heat a teaspoon of the oil in a large non-stick frying pan over a medium heat, then add both sausage patties. Fry on both sides for 4–5 minutes, or until they are cooked through, then set them aside. Keep the patties warm on a plate in the oven on a very low heat.

3. While the patties are cooking, grate the potato and parsnip with a cheese grater, then place them in a clean cloth or tea towel. Squeeze the tea towel as hard as you can over the sink or a large bowl to catch the excess liquid, until no further liquid comes out. Don't skip this step, or the hash browns will be soggy and less likely to bind together. Put the grated potato and parsnip into a large mixing bowl, then mix in the salt and pepper.

4. Heat the same frying pan with another teaspoon of oil and turn up the heat to medium-high. Once the oil is hot, spoon the hash brown mixture into two circular shapes. You can use greased egg or crumpet rings for neat hash browns, or shape them freestyle if you prefer.

5. Cook the hash browns for 3–4 minutes, then carefully flip them using a spatula or fish slice, and cook for a further 3–4 minutes on the other side. At this point, they should be golden and crispy on the outside, but if they are looking pale, cook for a further minute on both sides. Remove the hash browns from the pan, place them on the plate with the sausage patties, then return the plate to the oven to keep warm.

6. Add the remaining half teaspoon of oil to the frying pan. Once the oil is hot, crack the eggs directly into the pan, using greased egg rings if you like, then turn down the heat to low. Fry the eggs for 3 minutes, then check to see if the whites are cooked to your liking. If not, continue to fry for a further minute. You can also cover the pan with a lid to speed up the cooking time by steaming the top of the egg.

7. While the eggs are cooking, slice both muffins in half and toast them to your liking. Spread one half of each muffin with a teaspoon of cranberry sauce.

8. Place the muffin halves with the cranberry sauce on two plates. Add a sausage patty, hash brown and fried egg to each one, then sandwich them with the remaining toasted muffin halves. Serve immediately.

INDEX

ACKNOWLEDGEMENTS

Thank you to my family and friends for their love and encouragement, for listening to me talk endlessly about breakfast and, of course, for being the guinea pigs for my recipes!

A big thank you to the amazing team at HarperCollins for bringing this book to life and for creating such a fantastic design. My thanks in particular to Anna Mrowiec, my lovely editor, as well as Sarah Hammond and Julia Pollacco for all of their help throughout the process, and to Oli Malcolm for having the idea to commission the book in the first place. It really is a dream come true!

Finally, and most importantly, thank you to all of my wonderful fellow breakfast lovers who have supported me on Instagram and other social media since I posted my very first breakfast idea in 2015. This book would not be possible without you.